lonely planet

POCKET

PERTH & FREMANTLE

TOP SIGHTS • LOCAL EXPERIENCES

CHARLES RAWLINGS-WAY,
FLEUR BAINGER

Contents

Wirin by Tjyllyungoo (Lance Chadd), Yagan Sq (p35), Central Perth

Explore Perth & Fremantle 29

Worth a Trip

Survival Guide 149

Special Features

Welcome to Perth & Fremantle

Way out west in the Indian Ocean breeze, Perth is the most isolated city of its size on the planet. But this remoteness fosters a free-spirited, outward-looking world view: Perth and its port suburb Fremantle are uncomplicated, unfettered and alive. The city also offers superb beaches, global eats and booming small-bar and street-art scenes. Forget about isolation: Perth is going places!

Elizabeth Quay (p38), Central Perth
RUDY BALASKO / SHUTTERSTOCK ©

Top Sights

Kings Park

One of the world's largest inner-city parks. **p94**

Fremantle Prison

Fremantle's most frightening place is a World Heritage–listed wonder. **p122**

WA Shipwrecks Museum

Shipwrecks and stories of those lost at sea. **p126**

Cottesloe Beach

Towering Norfolk Island pines back Perth's prettiest beach. **p106**

Art Gallery of Western Australia

Perth's premier art gallery is a must-see. **p54**

Rottnest Island

A car-free holiday haven (and home to quokkas), not far offshore. **p144**

Scarborough Beach

Perth's version of Venice Beach. **p108**

Swan River

This broad river estuary both divides and defines the city. **p32**

Swan Valley

This glorious wine valley is just a day trip up the Swan River. **p48**

Western Australian Museum – Maritime

Explore Western Australia's inexorable ties with the sea. **p124**

Eating

Hungry? Of course you are. Perth chefs draw on culinary influences form across the Indian Ocean: pubs here are just as likely to have a lamb rogan josh curry on the menu as a porterhouse steak or chicken Parmigiana. Cafes here are reliably good, as are seafood restaurants, modern Australian (Mod Oz) bistros, burger bars and bakeries.

Where to Eat

Perth's neighbourhoods have different ways of doing food, but look forward to some cool cafes, brilliant bakeries and top seafood across the board. Leederville's Oxford St has too many good cafes to ignore, while Central Perth is awash with high-end bistros. Fremantle approaches appetite from a budget perspective, with excellent fish and chips. Northbridge is home to big burgers and quick-fire Asian joints, while from Scarborough to Cottesloe you can get decent pub meals and cafe lunches. Highgate, Mount Lawley and Subiaco have a bit of everything: bistros, cafes and wine bars with tempting menus.

Cheap Eats

The slowing of WA's resources boom means that Perth's restaurant prices have eased a little. However, it can still be an expensive city for the hungry.

For budget eats, head to the Little Asia section of William St in Northbridge, north of the main pub-and-club action. Most city shopping centres have food courts that are good for cheap noodles, sushi or a curry, and pubs often do good-value lunch specials. Many restaurants are BYO, meaning you can bring your own wine, though a corkage fee usually applies (even for screw-tops). Perth's excellent cafes are generally primed to deliver big breakfasts for under $20.

TAFFPIXTURE/SHUTTERSTOCK ©

Best Cafes

Mary Street Bakery Brilliant baked bits and chocolate-filled in Mt Lawley. (p77)

Sayers Sister Chorizo! Who doesn't like chorizo? Big Northbridge breakfasts. (p75)

Canvas Freo's best breakfasts are at the Fremantle Arts Centre's in-house cafe. (p132)

La Veen Need some baked eggs before your big meeting? (p43)

Ootong & Lincoln A top cafe in boho South Fremantle. Order the macadamia-and-*dukkah* porridge. (p134)

Best Modern Australian

Wildflower Rooftop wonderment at one of Perth's best restaurants (loud renditions of classic-rock hits by the Cult not recommended). (p40)

Balthazar Down near Elizabeth Quay, Balthazar is the effortlessly cool embodiment of new-century Perth fine dining. (p42)

St Michael 6003 Degustation delights at this Highgate highlight, with special seafood and serene, stylish service. (p75)

Bathers Beach House Fine Mod Oz dining needn't be haughty: down by the beach in Fremantle, it's anything but. (p133)

Best Self-Catering

Chez Jean-Claude Patisserie Brioche and baguettes to take away, all handled with French aplomb. (p100)

Perth City Farm Organic eggs, fruit, vegetables and bread, plus an excellent cafe (...come on, just one coffee – there'll be plenty of time for self-catering later on). (p43)

Kailis Bros Expect photogenic displays of fresh seafood and a cafe at the Leederville branch of this iconic seafood business. (Pictured; p88)

Kakulas Bros Fabulous deli and provisions shop in Northbridge; there's another branch in Fremantle. (p63)

Drinking & Nightlife

Recent law changes in Perth produced a salvo of quirky small bars that have been sprouting everywhere, including in the formerly deserted-after-dark CBD. Northbridge, traditionally pubby, brawly and brassy, now sustains a more idiosyncratic drinking scene, while in Fremantle – a hard-drinking port town – craft beer reigns supreme.

Sunday Sessions

They're not as popular now as they were a decade ago, but Perth drinkers still like to get wobbly on a Sunday afternoon, putting away plenty o' beers to finish out the weekend in style. 'Sunday Sessions' are advertised everywhere – it would be remiss of you not to attend at least one. And hey, you're on holiday – Monday morning means nothing to you!

Northbridge Nights

Northbridge dwells on the rough edge of Perth's nightlife, with countless pubs, strip joints and clubs around William and James Sts. After dark, tattooed, muscled-up 'roid boys in T-shirts seem permanently on the brink of violence, while scantily clad, vacant-looking girls try not to seem impressed. A harsh and unbalanced critique, probably – and some recent openings have certainly lifted the tone here. But on Saturday nights when fly-in/fly-out workers come to blow off steam, Northbridge can turn ugly very quickly. Still, this is where the fun is! Most pubs have lockouts, so you'll need to be in before midnight. Bring ID.

Best Craft Beer

Northbridge Brewing Company Something different for Northbridge: big beers and big screens aplenty. (p66)

Little Creatures Down on the Fremantle waterfront, one of Australia's original craft-beer breweries is still going strong. Great staff; even better food. (Pictured; p137)

Five Bar Craft beer is done with class in Mount Lawley. (p79)

Norfolk Hotel Fremantle's (and Perth's?) most

DAVID SUTHERLAND/ALAMY STOCK PHOTO ©

charming old pub has plenty of interesting taps with which to rend yourself crafty. (p138)

Dutch Trading Co South-side beers (very few of them Dutch) on an emerging strip across the bridge from East Perth. (p44)

Best Wine & Whisky

Helvetica Beyond a secret downtown doorway off Howard St, Helvetica does a mean whisky sour. (p45)

Varnish on King Vanish into Varnish on King St for 200 American whiskeys (you don't have to try them all in one session). (p45)

Must Winebar Must Winebar is a Mount Lawley must, with 40-odd wines by the glass and just as much class. (p79)

Alabama Song We doubt that Jim Morrison ever made it to Perth's CBD, but this whiskey bar would have been right up his alley. (p65)

Swallow A bit French, a bit art deco, little Swallow on the edge of Mount Lawley is a divine spot in which to swallow some Western Australian wine. (p78)

Best Small Bars

Sneaky Tony's Sneak into Tony's hidden Northbridge speakeasy with a secret password. Cocktails ahoy. (p65)

LOT 20 Emblematic of the new Northbridge: a small bar with charm and sophistication to burn. (p65)

Strange Company Drinking cool cocktails and WA craft brews in Freo ain't so strange. (p138)

Pinchos Little Leederville tapas bar with Spanish beer, wine, sherry and sangria. (p87)

Ezra Pound Bookish bohemia meets city-side cool at this Northbridge alleyway haunt. (p66)

Shopping

Over the years, few people have been heard to say, 'I'm going to Perth to experience world-class shopping!' Life here has always been more about the beach than the boutique. Perth still largely follows Sydney and Melbourne's lead when it comes to fashion, but there are some great markets and speciality shops, with Aboriginal art particularly well represented.

FARRIS NOORZALI/SHUTTERSTOCK ©

Shopping in the City

The shopping in Central Perth revolves around and between the Hay St Mall and Murray St Mall – parallel pedestrian zones lined with speciality shops, department stores, surf shops, trashy souvenir joints, cafes and supermarkets. Classier complexes like Forrest Chase (www.forrestchase.com.au) and Carillon City (www.carilloncity.com.au) run off the malls, hosting boutiques, jewellers and gift shops. Nearby, King St is the place for independent clothing designer outlets. Online, have a look at www.visitperth.com.au/see-and-do/shopping-areas for more on the various shopping precincts, malls and arcades around the city centre.

...and in the Suburbs

Further afield, the bottom end of High St in Fremantle plays host to interesting and quirky stores, while fashion shops run along Market St. Queen Victoria St in North Fremantle is the place to go for antiques. Leederville and Mount Lawley feature more eclectic shops; in particular, Leederville's Oxford St is the place for boutiques, eclectic music and bookshops. If you're after vintage or retro style, head to Northbridge. Meanwhile in Subiaco, Hay St and Rokeby Rd (pronounced 'rock-uh-bee', not 'roke-bee') boast fashion, art and classy gifts.

When to Shop

Shops in Perth and Fremantle keep fairly

EA GIVEN/SHUTTERSTOCK ©

regular hours: 9am to 5pm Monday to Saturday and around 11am to 5pm on Sunday. But in Central Perth there's late-night shopping on Fridays, most shops staying open until 9pm to catch the last of the city workers as they wander off towards the weekend. Note that the iconic Fremantle Markets complex is only open on Friday, Saturday and Sunday.

Best for Books & Music

Boffins Books A catchy name and an impressive collection of scientific, technical and specialist books and travel guides (look for the ones with the funky logo and the blue spine). (p47)

New Edition Australian literature has never been in a stronger position: settle into an armchair with something engaging from celebrated WA writers like Tim Winton or Robert Drewe. (p142)

Planet Books With all that sunshine outside, it's a wonder that Perth locals have the time or inclination to read books. Here's where they buy them. (p81)

Record Finder Divine vinyl in Fremantle. (p142)

Mills Records Another excellent Fremantle record shop, with a section dedicated to Freo and WA musos. (p143)

Best Markets

Fremantle Markets Freo's famous market sheds are full of weird arts and crafts, crappy souvenirs and much-better food and drink. Even if you don't buy anything, it's well worth a wander. (Pictured; p132)

Boatshed Market Fab food piled high, not far inland from Cottesloe Beach. (p118)

Subiaco Farmers Market Street eats, organic produce and family entertainment. (p100)

Beaches

Perth's western suburbs front directly onto the Indian Ocean – a long string of golden sand mirroring Sydney's Northern Beaches on the other side of the continent. Life by beach is chilled-out and unhurried, wed to breaking waves and ebbing tides. On any day of the week, Perth's beaches are full of people (don't they have jobs to do?).

Beach Bods

Australians hate to think of themselves as prudish or conservative – something to do with Irish stock and a healthy disrespect for authority. But on Perth's beaches, even the most open-minded Melburnian may find cause to blush. G-string bikinis are *de rigueur,* muscle-bound gym bods oil themselves to a lustrous sheen, and nobody is anybody without a tattoo or 12. This is the West. This is freedom. This is the Perth beach – sexed-up, confident and self-adulating.

Swim Between the Flags

Every year in Australia, thousands of people are dragged from the surf by surf-lifesavers, coughing up seaweed and gasping for air after being caught in a rip or dumped by a wave. Sadly, many (if not most) of these soggy souls are tourists, and not all of them survive. Play it safe beyond the shore: always swim between the red-and-yellow flags, never swim alone and never turn your back on the waves. In Perth, the Indian Ocean may look warm and inviting, but it can be a spiteful and tumultuous sea.

Best for Swimming

Sorrento Beach Forget about things that bite: Sorrento's big net keeps the big fish at bay. (p115)

Mettams Pool Between Trigg Beach and Sorrento Beach is this little-known snorkelling spot that's lovely for a dip. (p115)

Swanbourne Beach Get natural at Swanbourne, Perth's unofficial gay and nude beach. (p115)

BMPHOTOGRAPHER/SHUTTERSTOCK ©

South Beach Fremantle's beaches nearer the port tend to get a bit soupy: head to South Beach (further south) for a cleaner oceanic experience. (p134)

Best for Surfing

Scarborough Beach Scarborough rivals Cottesloe for beach culture, but the essence of 'Scarbs' remains the surf. If you're in need of a lesson, you're in the right place. (p108)

Floreat Beach Probably Perth's least crowded stretch of sand: if you're looking for some solo beach time, you'll find it here. (p116)

Trigg Beach Trigg surfers don't mess around: when the surf is pumping here, the local crew knows how to carve it up. (p116)

Best Beach Culture

Cottesloe Beach Cottesloe has it all: a gorgeous beach, safe swimming areas, good waves, a historic surf-club building, waterside pubs, backpackers and beautiful people. (Pictured; p106)

Bathers Beach WA's only beach with an alcohol licence – sundowners on the sand! If you can think of a better end to a Fremantle day, let us know. (p133)

City Beach Far enough from both Scarborough and Cottesloe to beat the crowds, City Beach has some fab cafes in which to contemplate another swim. (p114)

Beach Background

Run by the Surf Life Saving Club of WA, www.mybeach.com.au has a profile of all Perth's beaches, including weather forecasts and information about buses, amenities and beach patrols. Handy stuff to know.

Aboriginal Art & Culture

Around 77,000 Aboriginal people call WA home, comprising many different Indigenous peoples, speaking many distinct languages. Perth is Wadjuk country, part of the broader Noongar nation who call southewestern WA home. In the city you'll find plenty of places to see and buy Aboriginal art, plus some informative and enlightening cultural tours run by local Wadjuk guides.

T. M. YUSOF/ALAMY STOCK PHOTO © ARTWORK BY NYOONGAR ARTISTS

Buying Aboriginal Art – Ethically

Make sure what you're buying is the real deal and that your money goes to the right people: buy directly from galleries and outlets that are owned and operated, or supported, by Indigenous communities. The Indigenous Art Code (www.indigenousartcode.org) lists galleries considered to observe ethical practices. Artworks themselves should also have a certificate of authenticity. Note, too, that haggling is not part of Aboriginal culture.

Best Aboriginal Art

Japingka An ethically attuned Fremantle dealer, specialising in high-end product. (p142)

Mossenson Galleries – Indigenart Gorgeous weavings, paintings and sculpted works from across the country come to Subiaco. (p103)

Aboriginal Art & Craft Gallery Duck into this interesting commercial gallery in Kings Park. (p103)

Art Gallery of Western Australia A treasure trove of Indigenous art. (p54)

Best Cultural Tours

Djurandi Dreaming Aboriginal cultural walking tours around Elizabeth Quay precinct in Central Perth. (p38)

Go Cultural Aboriginal Tours Small-group walking tours around the new Yagan Sq precinct, and Elizabeth Quay. (p40)

Active Outdoors

DAVID STEELE/SHUTTERSTOCK ©

It does rain here, but not often! Actually, Perth is wetter than Adelaide, Hobart and Melbourne – but when the WA sun is shining, there are few more pleasant places to be than the city's parks, plazas and walking trails. Pack a picnic, head outside and get active. If you're not the outdoors type already, you soon will be!

Best Parks

Kings Park Offering brilliant views of the city and lengthy walking trails, Kings Park is a Perth essential. Don't miss the lofty 620m Lotterywest Federation Walkway. (Pictured; p102)

Hyde Park Navigate the path around the lake at one of Perth's prettiest parks, in leafy Mount Lawley. (p75)

Esplanade Reserve Lined with Norfolk Island pines, Fremantle's waterside park is a hub for families, skaters, picnickers and protesters. (p133)

Lake Monger Near Leederville, the parklands around Lake Monger have jogging trails and open space aplenty. (p87)

Best by the River

Elizabeth Quay The plazas and walkways around redeveloped Elizabeth Quay connect the Swan River with Central Perth: this really is a river city! (p38)

Bicton Baths Low-key suburban swims at this lovely little riverside park. (p33)

Spinway WA Hire a bike in the CBD and go exploring: trails meander along the the Swan River's banks from the city centre and back again. (p152)

Best by the Beach

Scarborough Beach Pool If the beach is too windy (or even if it isn't), Scarborough's gorgeous 50m foreshore pool is irresistible. (p116)

Coastal Trail Tracking right along Perth's suburban coast, this endless cycling/walking trail is eternally popular. (p116)

Snake Pit Take the drop into this 3.6m-deep concrete skate bowl on the Scarborough Beach foreshore. (p117)

Fun's Back Surf Hire a surfboard or a stand-up paddleboard and splash into the Cottesloe brine. (p115)

With Kids

EA GIVEN/SHUTTERSTOCK ©

Kids either like somewhere, or they don't! There's usually not a lot of grey area... But if we must, yes, Perth is a very kid-friendly city, with daredevil activities, interesting museums, splashy water parks and wild critters to meet. And more often than not, the sun is shining!

Best Places to Cool Off

Hyde Park Playground Excellent suburban water park (free!), with splashy jets aplenty. (p75)

Elizabeth Quay Water Park Down by the river at vamped-up Elizabeth Quay, kids run amok through free fountains. (Pictured; p35)

Beatty Park Leisure Centre Perth's 1962 Commonweath Games swimming pool is still buckets of fun. (p87)

Best Museums & Galleries

Fremantle Arts Centre Fabulously arty programs, performances and activities for kids. (p132)

WA Shipwrecks Museum Kids and shipwrecks – the fascination is never-ending. (p126)

Scitech Excellent push-button/pull-lever science interaction aimed squarely at kids. (p100)

Best Creature Encounters

Perth Zoo Perth Zoo is shady, compact and marvellously well laid-out – it's a pleasure to push a pram around here! (p38)

Aquarium of Western Australia Traverse underwater tunnels and eyeball WA's myriad underwater residents. (p114)

Camel West Camels? In the city? Yes indeed. Make friends with one as you ride along the riverfront. (p40)

Worth a Trip

Out near the airport, iFly Indoor Skydiving (www.ifly.com.au) lets the kids fly in a surging column of air! Similarly gravity-defying are the water slides and roller coasters at Adventure World (www.adventureworld.net.au) south of town.

LGBTIQ+

Like all big Australian cities these days, Perth is largely a welcoming and safe destination for gay and lesbian travellers. The scene here is a lot smaller than on the east coast (it's hard to compete with Sydney!), but Perth does have a few top-shelf bars, clubs and drag shows. And if you're in town in November, don't miss the fabulous PrideFest.

ALEXANDER_H_SCHULZ/GETTY IMAGES ©

Where to Go

Perth is home to all of Western Australia's gay and lesbian venues, with the scene squarely centred on Northbridge. But before you get too excited, let's clarify matters: 'all of WA's gay and lesbian venues' entails a couple of bars, a club, and one men's sauna. It's hardly what you'd call a pumping scene... But fear not: many other bars, especially around Highgate and Mt Lawley, are entirely gay-friendly. It's unlikely you'll experience any real problems, although the late-night Northbridge vibe can be a tad redneck at times. In November, don't miss the extravagant 10-day **PrideFest** (www.pridewa.com.au; ⏲Nov).

Useful resources:

Pride Western Australia (www.pridewa.com.au) has statewide listings and happenings.

For a heads-up on what's on, pick up Out in Perth (www.outinperth.com), a free monthly newspaper.

Q Pages (www.qpages.com.au) has a gay and lesbian business directory and what's-on listings.

Living Proud (www.livingproud.org.au) is an information and counselling line.

Best LGBTIQ+ Perth

The Court Myriad bars, dance floors and drag shows aplenty. (p66)

Hula Bula Bar Go 'South Pacific' in this Polynesian-themed bar. (p45)

Connections Perth's main gay club, with DJs, drag shows and a great rooftop bar. (p66)

Perth Steam Works Gay sauna just north of the Northbridge strip. (p61)

Four Perfect Days

FLEUR BAINGER/LONELY PLANET ©

Kick off your Perth explorations with a leisurely cafe breakfast on Beaufort St in **Mt Lawley** (p71) or **Central Perth** (p31), then spend your first morning exploring the Perth Cultural Centre in Northbridge – don't miss the superb **Art Gallery of Western Australia** (p54) and the **Western Australian Museum – Perth** (p60), which, by the time you read this, will have rebranded as the New Museum for Western Australia. Grab lunch and browse the shops in hip **Leederville** (pictured; p83) before exploring verdant, view-catching **Kings Park** (p94) – one of the biggest urban parks on the planet. Trundle down Rokeby Rd for dinner and brinks in nearby **Subiaco** (p93).

TRAVELSCAPE IMAGES/ALAMY STOCK PHOTO ©; *SPANDA* BY CHRISTIAN DE VIETRI

The following day, discover the lustrous riches of the **Perth Mint** (p39) before catching the **Little Ferry Co** (p152) from **Elizabeth Quay** (pictured; p38) to check out the city from the shimmering **Swan River** (p32). A night drinking cocktails in the city laneway bars, or bouncing between craft-beer boltholes and boozy pubs in **Northbridge** (p53) awaits. If you're in luck you might catch a live troubadour or two. Perth's compact Chinatown is here too (and 'Little Asia' on William St; north of the main pub-and-club action) for a late-night, quick-fire laksa, a steaming plate of noodles or some dumplings.

Day 3

FLEUR BAINGER/LONELY PLANET ©

Time to hit the beach. Pick up provisions for a picnic at **Cottesloe** (pictured; p106), with its golden sands, swaying Norfolk Island pines and safe swimming, or truck further north to the booming **Scarborough** (p108) foreshore, with its brilliant outdoor swimming pool, precipitous skate bowl and rolling surf (and surf lessons). Not in a beachy state of mind? Catch a ferry to history-rich **Rottnest Island** (p144) and go exploring on a bike (OK, so the beaches here are good too!); or take a tour of the nearby **Swan Valley** (p48) to taste some fine WA wine and gourmet goodies (the craft beer is bountiful here too).

Day 4

RICHARD CUMMINS/ALAMY STOCK PHOTO ©, *MEMORIAL TO THE MIGRANT CHILDREN* BY SMITH SCULPTORS

On your final day, visit **Fremantle**: Perth's raffish, atmospheric port enclave. Bookshops, buskers and bars: 'Freo' has soul! Two of WA's best museums are on hand – the sea-salty **Western Australian Museum – Maritime** (pictured; p124) and **WA Shipwrecks Museum** (p126) – plus the disquieting, World Heritage–listed **Fremantle Prison** (p122), which served as a lock-up as recently as 1991. Take your pick, then conclude your Perth adventure with some chilly pints at **Little Creatures** (p137), still one of Australia's best breweries.

Need to Know

For detailed information, see Survival Guide p149

Currency
Australian dollar ($)

Language
English

Visas
All visitors to Australia need a visa (except New Zealanders). Apply at www.homeaffairs.gov.au.

Money
ATMs are plentiful, and there are currency-exchange facilities at the airport and major banks in the CBD.

Mobile Phones
Australia's mobile network is compatible with most European phones, but generally not with the US or Japanese systems.

Time
Australian Western Standard Time (GMT/UTC plus eight hours).

Tipping
Tipping is not mandatory in WA, but 10% is appropriate for excellent restaurant service.

Daily Budget

Budget: Less than $150

Dorm bed in a hostel: $30–50

Private hostel room: $80–130

Mainly self-catering, with the occasional budget meal: $30

Public transport DayRider pass: $12.80

Midrange: $150–350

Double room in a midrange hotel: $130–250

Lunch in a cafe or pub: $30–40

River cruise or surf lesson: $40–70

Short taxi ride: $20

Top End: More than $350

Double room in a top hotel: from $250

Three-course dinner in a top restaurant: over $80

Car rental per day: $50

Advance Planning

- Check what kind of visa you'll need to visit Australia.
- Check that your passport has at least six months' validity.
- If you're flying into Perth, check which terminal you'll be landing at: there are four, with different domestic/international transfer and public transport considerations.
- Bring a 'rashie' swimming top, a broad-rim hat and sunglasses to combat the sun on Perth's glorious beaches.

Arriving in Perth

From Perth Airport

Perth Airport is 10km east of Perth. Rent a car, or jump in a taxi (around $45 into the city) or prebooked shuttle bus (from $25).

From Elizabeth Quay Bus Station

South West Coach Lines focuses on WA's southwestern corner, with buses departing Elizabeth Quay.

From East Perth Station

Transwa runs trains and buses into rural WA from East Perth. Great Southern Rail runs the *Indian Pacific* train between Perth and Sydney, also departing East Perth.

Getting Around

Car

There are local and international car-rental offices at the airport and in the city.

Train

Transperth operates five lines: Armadale, Thornlie, Fremantle, Joondalup, Mandurah and Midland.

Bus

Regular Transperth buses and free Central Area Transit (CAT) buses service the city. Fremantle also has free CAT bus services.

Taxi

Metered taxis abound: hail one by by raising your arm, or head for a taxi rank. Uber operates in Perth.

Ferry

Ferry across the Swan River from Elizabeth Quay to Mends St Jetty in South Perth (for Perth Zoo).

Perth & Fremantle Neighbourhoods

Scarborough to Cottesloe (p105)
Perth's beach suburbs adhere to a string of glorious Indian Ocean beaches. Look forward to pubs, seafood eateries and surf lessons.

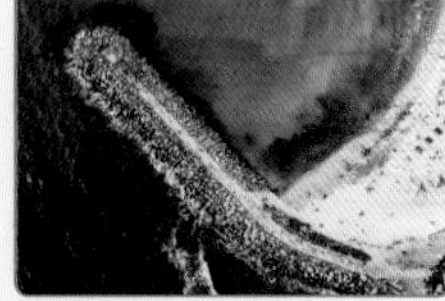

Fremantle (p121)
This arty, atmospheric harbour hood is a Perth essential, with outstanding museums and fab eating and drinking.

Scarborough Beach

Cottesloe Beach

Western Australian Museum – Maritime

Fremantle Prison

WA Shipwrecks Museum

Leederville (p83)
Spend a day drifting between cafes, bars and restaurants in bohemian Leederville, not far north of Central Perth.

Highgate & Mount Lawley (p71)
Refined inner-city neighbourhoods with lovely parks, wine bars, cafes, bakeries and interesting architecture.

Swan Valley

Northbridge (p53)
Perth's nocturnal playground is fun, edgy and progressive, with an ever-evolving list of bars and multicultural eats. The Art Gallery of Western Australia is here too.

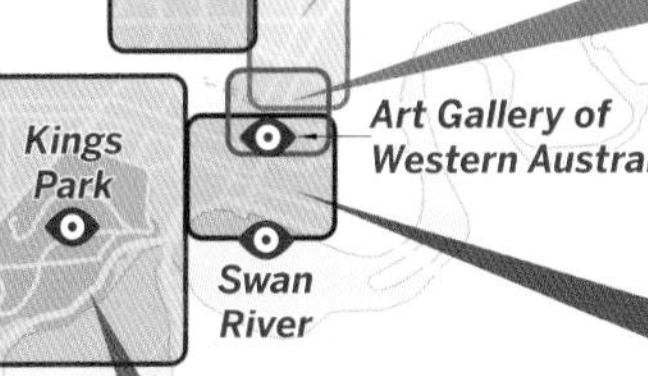

Central Perth (p31)
In among the concrete canyons, Central Perth has some terrific places to eat and drink, and access to the Swan River.

Kings Park & Subiaco (p93)
One of the world's biggest urban parks next to a food-focused inner-city enclave: what a perfect pairing!

Explore
Perth & Fremantle

Worth a Trip

Perth & Fremantle's Walking Tours

Elizabeth Quay Bridge (p38), Central Perth
BENNYMARTY/GETTY IMAGES ©; ARCHITECT: ARUP ASSOCIATES

Explore Central Perth

Perth's soaring city centre is a glam architectural salute to the economic wave that Western Australia has surfed in recent decades. But in among the glass and steel are some gorgeous heritage buildings and excellent places to eat and drink, while the shimmering Swan River provides a timeless reminder that this place has always been 'Mooro' on Wadjuk land.

The Short List

- ***Bell Tower (p38)*** *Climbing this towering contemporary edifice.*
- ***Perth Zoo (p38)*** *Ferrying over to Perth's brilliantly laid-out zoo.*
- ***Elizabeth Quay (p38)*** *Exploring this hive of ferry, food and family activity linking Central Perth with the Swan River.*
- ***Downtown drinking (p43)*** *Hopping between brilliant bars and craft-beer emporia.*
- ***Perth Mint (p39)*** *Feeding your greed at this shrine to the mighty dollar.*

Getting There & Around

Perth's five train lines converge in Central Perth, terminating at either Perth, Perth Underground or Elizabeth Quay stations.

Buses run into Central Perth from the places the trains can't reach: reliable and frequent, but time consuming.

If you're staying anywhere off a train or bus route, jump in a cab.

Neighbourhood Map on p36

Spanda by Christian de Vietri, Elizabeth Quay (p38)

Top Sight

Swan River

The Swan River cuts through the core of Perth, splitting the city into north and south and providing oodles of waterfront for locals who choose river over sea. It's where ferries journey to Fremantle and on to Rottnest, where yachts cruise and catamarans jibe, where dolphins bob and kayaks skim. On windy days, you might even see wind- and kitesurfers. The river is very swimmable, with grassy shores perfect for picnicking.

MAP P36, E6

www.experienceperth.com/destination/swan-river

River City

When you think of the world's great river cities – New Orleans, Prague, Paris, Varanasi, Memphis – Perth may not readily spring to mind. Even within Australia, Melbourne, Brisbane and Hobart have traditionally embraced their rivers more passionately. But make no mistake: the Swan River is Perth's lifeblood and its social pacemaker (do you live north, south or right on the river?). And now, the redevelopment of Elizabeth Quay (p38) has turned a new page in the story of Central Perth and its waterway: interesting cafes, hotels, apartment towers, bars, restaurants and the striking Elizabeth Quay bridge (pictured left) are bringing people back to the riverfront, while the bus, train and ferry hubs here deliver commuters into Central Perth. Perth's future as a great river city has taken a giant step forwards.

Rollin' on the River

Perth locals are up and about early, jogging and cycling along the riverbanks, swimming and stand-up paddleboarding. Join their ranks with these riverine activities:

Water Wanderers (p40) Guided and self-guided kayak tours around the Swan.

Little Ferry Co (p39) Chug between the Elizabeth Quay and Claisebrook Cove.

Bicton Baths (☎ 08-9364 0666; www.melvillecity.com.au; 80 Blackwall Reach Pde, Bicton; admission free; ⏲ daylight hours; 👪) A lovely neighbourhood saltwater-swim spot.

★ Top Tips

- Take a ferry trip along the river; numerous companies depart from Elizabeth Quay.
- Hire a bike and cycle the 10km loop along the Esplanade, over the Narrows Bridge and along the South Perth foreshore. Stop at Heirisson Island at dusk and spot wild but friendly kangaroos (they hide during the heat of the day).
- Look out for dolphins as you're picnicking; Matilda Bay is deservedly popular, while Chidley Point and Freshwater Bay are local favourites.

✕ Take a Break

- **Bayside Kitchen** (www.facebook.com/baysidematildabay) at Matilda Bay combines gorgeous views with an elevated cafe for casual, good-value dishes.
- For something more upmarket (and pricey), head to **Matilda Bay Food and Wine** (www.matildabayrestaurant.com.au).

Walking Tour

Central Perth Old & New

Bookended by two of Perth's newly revitalised precincts – Yagan Sq, connecting the CBD with neighbouring Northbridge; and Elizabeth Quay, connecting the CBD with the Swan River – this walk highlights the evolution of Central Perth. Gorgeous architectural remnants crop up along the way – Central Perth is older than it looks!

Walk Facts

Start Yagan Sq; Perth Station

End Elizabeth Quay; Elizabeth Quay Station

Length 4km; two hours

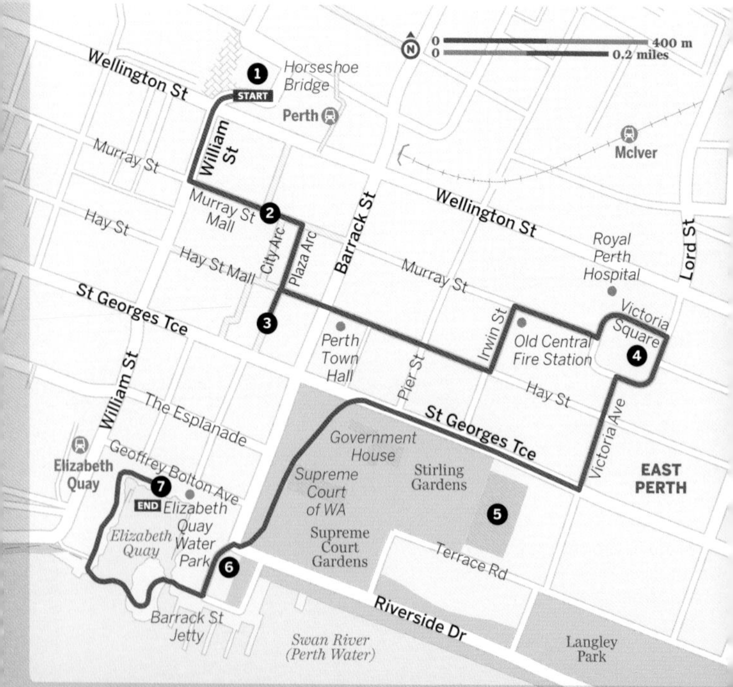

❶ Yagan Sq

Get started at **Yagan Sq**, held within the embrace of the historic Horseshoe Bridge, above the rail lines. Named in honour of Yagan, a Wadjuk warrior upon whose land Perth now stands, this public space is fast becoming the social hub of the city.

❷ Murray St Mall

Cross Wellington St, head south down William St and turn left onto buzzy **Murray St Mall**, the city's main shopping precinct. Cut through the art-deco Plaza Arcade to Hay St Mall, more low-key than its Murray St partner in commerce.

❸ London Court

Nearby, you'll spy the marvellously over-the-top **London Court** (www.londoncourt.com.au), a mock-Elizabethan shopping arcade built in 1937. Backtrack and turn right to the corner of Hay St Mall and Barrack St where the beautifully restored Town Hall (1870) soars high, with its impressive clock tower.

❹ St Mary's Cathedral

Continue up Hay St and turn left up Irwin St. At the corner of Irwin and Murray Sts is the Old Central Fire Station (1901). Turn right onto Murray St: you'll pass the red-brick Royal Perth Hospital en route to the 1863 **St Mary's Cathedral** (Victoria Sq) at the end of the street.

❺ Perth Concert Hall

Do a lap around Victoria Square then track south to the Perth Concert Hall (p47), a grand auditorium on St Georges Tce cobbled together in the early 1970s. Continue west along St Georges Tce past turreted Government House (1864) then dart through Stirling Gardens to the noble Supreme Court (1903).

❻ Bell Tower

Wind south of the Supreme Court and make for the river. Within moments the Bell Tower (p38) will come into view: controversial when it was built in 1999, it's become a must-see viewpoint for visitors to the city.

❼ Elizabeth Quay

Around the corner is fast-evolving Elizabeth Quay (p38). Wander across the pedestrian bridge and survey the scene: cafes, bars, ferries, gondolas, kids, tourists...this is the new Perth!

Elizabeth Quay Water Park

Cool your boots after your walk at this free waterside **splash park** (Map p36, C5; ☎08-6557 0700; www.mra.wa.gov.au; Geoffrey Bolton Way; admission free; ⏰10am-10pm daily Dec-Feb, to 6pm Wed-Mon Mar-Nov; 👪), a curvy sunken terrace with water jets squirting upwards for 50 minutes every hour (on the hour). The kids love it!

For reviews see

Top Sights	p32
Sights	p38
Eating	p40
Drinking	p43
Entertainment	p46
Shopping	p47

E
F
G
H
Weld Sq
Aberdeen St
Francis St
Parry St
Newcastle St
Beaufort St
Stirling St
Pier St
Nash St
Aberdeen St
Lord St
Graham Farmer Fwy
25
1
17
Lime St
2
James St
McIver
Royal St
Hill St
Barrack St
Moore St
Wellington St
Witenoom St
Lord St
Moore St
Hill St
3
Wellington Sq
14
13
Murray St
Royal Perth Hospital
Victoria
Wellington St
Pier St
EAST PERTH
Hay St
Square
Goderich St
Irwin St
4
Goderich St
St Georges Tce
Victoria Ave
23
Hill St
Perth Mint
4
Government House
Hay St
Stirling Gardens
29
Victoria Ave
5
Governor's Ave
Terrace Rd
Hill St
Burt Way
St Georges Tce
30
Dutch Trading Co (2.5km)
Bennett St
Terrace Rd
Swan River
Langley Park
6
Riverside Dr
E
F
G
H

Sights

Elizabeth Quay

AREA

1 MAP P36, C5

A vital part of the city's urban redevelopment is Elizabeth Quay, at the bottom of Barrack St. Luxury hotels and apartments – including the Ritz – are nearing completion, joining waterfront cafes and restaurants. With a busport, train station and ferry terminal, the area is also a busy transport hub. Cross the spectacular Elizabeth Quay pedestrian bridge and splash in the water park. (www.elizabethquay.com.au; Barrack St)

Perth Zoo

ZOO

2 MAP P36, A5

Part of the fun is getting to this zoo – take a ferry across the Swan River from Elizabeth Quay Jetty (p152) to Mends St Jetty (every half-hour) and walk up the hill. Zones include Australian Bushwalk (kangaroos, emus, koalas, dingoes), Reptile Encounter (all those Aussie snakes you want to avoid), peaceful Australian Wetlands (black swans, brolgas, blue-billed ducks) and the usual international animals from giraffes and lions to elephants and orangutans. Another transport option is bus 30 or 31 from Elizabeth Quay Bus Station. (08-9474 0444; www.perthzoo.wa.gov.au; 20 Labouchere Rd; adult/child $32/15.50; 9am-5pm)

Bell Tower

LANDMARK

3 MAP P36, D5

This pointy glass spire fronted by copper sails contains the royal bells of London's St Martin-in-the-Fields, the oldest of which dates from 1550. The 12 bells were given to WA by the British government in 1988, and are the only set known to have left England. Clamber to the top for 360-degree views of Perth by the river. (08-6210 0444;

Aboriginal Walking Tours

Djurandi Dreaming (0458 692 455; www.djurandi.com.au; tours adult/child $45/35) offers tours around the booming Elizabeth Quay precinct in Central Perth. It's 45 minutes of Nyungar cultural immersion, focusing on stories of the Dreaming, art, native flora and fauna, traditional diet, seasons and family structures.

Go Cultural Aboriginal Tours (0459 419 778; www.gocultural.com.au) are small-group, Aboriginal-run tours of Yagan Sq (one hour, $40) and Elizabeth Quay (90 minutes, $60) in Central Perth. Tours peel back the layers of the city to understand the cultural and physical landscape of Aboriginal life here, now and in ancient times. Three-hour tours are also available ($120).

Perth Zoo

www.thebelltower.com.au; Barrack Sq; adult/child $18/9 incl bell-tower chiming experience; 10am-4pm, ringing noon-1pm Mon, Thu & Sun)

Perth Mint HISTORIC BUILDING

4 MAP P36, H4

Dating from 1899, the compelling Mint displays a collection of coins, nuggets and gold bars. You can caress bullion worth over $700,000, mint your own coins and watch gold pours (on the half-hour, from 9.30am to 3.30pm). The Mint's Gold Exhibition features a massive, Guinness World Record–holding 1 tonne gold coin, worth a staggering $60 million. (08-9421 7222; www.perthmint.com.au; 310 Hay St; adult/child $19/8; 9am-5pm)

Oh Hey WA WALKING

5 MAP P36, D4

Highly rated Central Perth walking tours, zeroing in on the city's booming street-art scene, hip small bars, throbbing nightlife zones and architectural heritage. Self-guided audio tours and two-hour bike tours also available. (0408 995 965; www.ohheywa.com.au; 45 St Georges Tce; tours from $35)

Little Ferry Co BOATING

6 MAP P36, C5

This heritage-style electric ferry travels between the Elizabeth Quay terminal and the cafes and restaurants of Claisebrook Cove – an excellent Swan River snapshot. Either take a return trip or bus

Water Wanderers

Guided and self-guided **kayak tours** (☎0412 101 949; www.waterwanderers.com.au) around the Swan River in Central Perth offer a watery perspective that most locals never experience. Tours run at dawn ($55, 75 minutes), in the morning ($60, 90 minutes) and at twilight ($79, two hours), departing from locations in South Perth and East Perth. Self-guided tours for experienced kayakers are $160 for two paddlers.

it back to the city on the free CAT bus. Also connects to Optus Stadium (p46) on big-game days. (☎0488 777 088; www.littleferryco.com.au; Elizabeth Quay; 1/2/3 stops adult $12/18/22, child $10/16/20, day pass adult/child $32/28; ⏲10am-5.30pm)

Camel West HORSE RIDING

7 MAP P36, D5

OK, so the idea of riding a camel in the middle of a major Australian city is a little odd...but without camels, the early white WA colonies would never have been able to trade and move goods from one remote point to another. Catch the humpy vibe on 30-minute waterfront ride, departing near Barrack St Jetty. (☎0437 404 037; www.camelwest.com.au; Riverside Dr; adult/child $45/30; ⏲10am-1pm Wed-Sun; 👪)

Eating

Petition Kitchen AUSTRALIAN $$

8 MAP P36, D4

One of Perth's most polished warehouse bistros, Petition manages to impress across all meal sittings with its inventive approach to local and seasonal ingredients, sometimes woven with indigenous produce such as finger lime or pepper berry. Breakfast is punchy, lunch wows with squid-ink linguine, pipis and Pernod, while dinner keeps the party going with charred zucchini, stracciatella and curry leaf. (☎08-6168 7771; www.petitionperth.com/kitchen; cnr St Georges Terrace & Barrack St; small plates $12-22, large plates $17-60; ⏲7am-11pm Mon-Fri, from 8am Sat & Sun; ❄)

Wildflower MODERN AUSTRALIAN $$$

9 MAP P36, D4

Filling a glass pavilion atop the restored State Buildings, Wildflower offers fine-dining menus inspired by the six seasons of the Indigenous Noongar people of WA. There's a passionate focus on WA produce: dishes often include Shark Bay scallops or kangaroo smoked over jarrah embers, as well as indigenous herbs and bush plants like lemon myrtle and wattle seed. (☎08-6168 7855; www.wildflowerperth.com.au; State Bldgs, 1 Cathedral Ave; mains $42-49, 5-course tasting menu without/with wine $145/240; noon-2.30pm & 6pm-late Tue-Fri, 6pm-late Sat)

Print Hall

MODERN AUSTRALIAN $$$

10 MAP P36, C3

This sprawling complex in the Brookfield Pl precinct includes the **Apple Daily**, featuring South-east Asian–style street food, the perfect-for-leaning **Print Hall Bar** and a swish Italian restaurant called **Gazette**. Don't miss having a drink and a burger or pizza in the rooftop **Bob's Bar**, named after Australia's larrikin former prime minister Bob Hawke. (08-6282 0000; www.printhall.com.au; 125 St Georges Tce; shared plates $12-20, mains $25-49; 11.30am-midnight Mon-Fri, from 4pm Sat)

Angel Falls Grill

VENEZUELAN $$

11 MAP P36, B2

The pick of Shafto Lane's ethnic restaurants, Angel Falls Grill brings a taste of South America to WA. Salads and meat dishes are served with arepas (flat breads), and starters include empanadas and savoury-topped plantains. Grilled meat dishes from the *parrillada* (BBQ) are flavour-packed, and surprising breakfast options also make Angel Falls a great place to start the day. (08-9481 6222; www.angelfallsgrill.com.au; Shop 16, Shafto Lane; mains $18-50; 11am-late)

Long Chim

THAI $$$

Australian chef David Thompson is renowned for respecting the authentic flavours of Thai

Long Chim

street food, and with dishes like a tongue-burning chicken *laap* (warm salad with fresh herbs) and roast red-duck curry, there's definitely no dialling back the flavour for Western palates. Find it next to Petition Kitchen (see 8 Map p36, D4). The prawns with toasted coconut and betel leaves may well be the planet's finest starter... (08-6168 7775; www.longchimperth.com; State Bldgs, cnr St Georges Tce & Barrack St; mains $25-45; noon-late;)

Balthazar

MODERN AUSTRALIAN $$$

12 MAP P36, D4

Low-lit, discreet and sophisticated, with a cool soundtrack and charming staff, Balthazar has an informal vibe that's matched by exquisite food and a famously excellent wine list. The menu is refreshingly original, combining European flavours with an intensely local and seasonal focus. Younger owners have reinvented Balthazar as a refined yet relaxed option with superior shared plates. (08-9421 1206; www.balthazar.com.au; 6 The Esplanade; small plates $21-28, large plates $36-57; noon-midnight Mon-Fri, from 6pm Sat)

Le Vietnam

VIETNAMESE $

13 MAP P36, E3

The best bánh mì (Vietnamese baguettes) in town are served in this tiny, central spot. Classic flavour combos blend pork slivers, pâté, chilli and lemongrass, while newer spins feature pulled pork, roast pork and crackling. Interesting drinks include Vietnamese coffee and lychee lemonade, and a hearty breakfast or lunch will only cost around 10 bucks. (08-6114 8038; www.facebook.com/levietnamcafe; 1/80 Barrack St; snacks $7; 7.30am-3pm Mon-Fri;)

Wadjuk Country

Too often excluded from Perth's race to riches have been the Wadjuk people, of the broader Noongar nation. In 2006 the Perth Federal Court recognised native title over the city of Perth and its surrounds, but this finding was appealed by the WA and Commonwealth governments. In December 2009 an agreement was signed in WA's parliament, setting out a time frame for negotiating settlement of native-title claims across the southwest. In mid-2015 a $1.3 billion native-title deal was settled by the WA government recognising the Noongar people as the traditional owners of WA's southwest. Covering over 200,000 sq km, the settlement region stretches from Jurien Bay to Ravensthorpe, and includes the Perth metropolitan area.

Santini Bar & Grill ITALIAN $$$

14 MAP P36, E3

Classy, fine-dining-style Italian food is served in the undeniably cool interiors of the **QT hotel** (www.qthotelsandresorts.com/perth). The pasta is made in-house (the duck 'Bolognese' with crackling is a thing of beauty), the fish is ocean-fresh (try the tuna crostini) and the perfectly seasoned steak sublime. The pizzas are cracking too. Have a pre or post drink across the hall. (08-9225 8000; www.santinibarandgrill.com.au; QT Perth, 133 Murray St; small plates $14-24, large plates $23-58; 6.30am-late;)

Lalla Rookh ITALIAN $$

15 MAP P36, D4

Escape down a hole in the CBD pavement to this subsurface restaurant specialising in modern Italian food. The fare encourages relaxed grazing with a tableful of shared dishes and local wine from the thoughtfully compiled wine list. Find the petite wine shop, down a side street, a hideaway serving the full menu. (08-9325 7077; www.lallarookh.com.au; lower ground fl, 77 St Georges Tce; pizza from $18, shared plates from $15; 11.30am-midnight Mon-Fri, from 5pm Sat)

La Veen CAFE $$

16 MAP P36, C2

La Veen's sunny brick-lined space, around the corner from fashion and design stores, showcases some of the city's best breakfast and lunch dishes – and it does excellent coffee. This being Australia, of course shakshuka (baked eggs) is on the menu, but La Veen's version, topped with dukkah and yogurt and served with ciabatta toast, is one of Perth's best. (08-9321 1188; www.laveencoffee.com.au; 90 King St; mains $13-25; 6.30am-3pm Mon-Fri, 7.30am-2pm Sat & Sun)

Perth City Farm MARKET $$

17 MAP P36, H2

Local organic producers sell eggs, fruit, vegetables and bread at the Saturday-morning markets, and there's an excellent cafe on-site from Monday to Saturday. It's interesting to roam the grounds, looking at the community-run veggie gardens. (08-9221 7300; www.perthcityfarm.org.au; 1 City Farm Pl; mains $13-21.50; 8am-noon Sat, cafe 7am-3pm Mon-Fri, to noon Sat)

Drinking

Petition Beer Corner CRAFT BEER

Distressed walls provide the backdrop for craft brews at this spacious bar around the corner from its kitchen counterpart (see 8 Map p36, D4). There's a rotating selection of 18 independent beers on tap – check out Now Tapped on Petition's website – and it's a great place to explore the more experimental side of the Australian craft-beer scene. Servings begin at just 150mL, so the curious beer fan will be in heaven. (08-6168 7773;

www.petitionperth.com/beer; State Bldgs, cnr St Georges Tce & Barrack St; 11.30am-late Mon-Sat, from noon Sun;)

Halford

COCKTAIL BAR

18 MAP P36, E4

Channelling a golden, 1950s vibe, basement bar Halford is where to come to sip Rat Pack–worthy cocktails, including expertly prepared martinis and other American bar classics. Halford's decor and furnishings combine theatre with a tinge of retro style too, with shimmering fabrics, coloured mood lighting, and vintage boxing pics lining the walls. (08-6168 7780; www.halfordbar.com.au; State Bldgs, cnr Hay St & Cathedral Ave; 4pm-2am Sat-Wed)

Southside Craft Beer

In an up-and-coming eating-and-drinking strip south of the river in Victoria Park, the **Dutch Trading Co** (see Map p36, H5; 08-6150 8329; www.thedutchtradingco.com.au; 243 Albany Hwy, Victoria Park; 4pm-midnight Tue-Thu, from noon Fri & Sat, to 10pm Sun) combines rustic bar-leaners and repurposed sofas with tattooed and bearded bartenders slinging the best of Aussie craft beers. Besides the ever-changing taps, there's a fridge full of international brews, and bar snacks include croquettes with mustard, spicy buttermilk chicken and hearty steak sandwiches.

Tiny's

BAR

19 MAP P36, A2

It's hard to decide if this is a bar with excellent food, or a restaurant with a strong booze focus. Tiny's blurs the lines beautifully, starting with a punchy cocktail program, a refined wine list and a fun wine shop; and continuing with the city's best rotisserie chicken (with gravy). It has cool factor in spades and gets raucous Fridays. (08-6166 9188; www.tinysbar.com.au; QV1 Plaza, cnr Hay St & Milligan St; 11.30am-late Mon-Fri, from 4pm Sat)

Alfred's Pizzeria

BAR

20 MAP P36, D4

Pizza by the slice at all hours, a dive-bar vibe (with a touch of *The Godfather*), and craft beer and Aussie wines all combine in this improbably compact space in the CBD. Check out the cool B&W photos of heritage NYC, and don't miss the wall-covering murals featuring Axl Rose as Jesus and Madonna as the Virgin Mary. (www.alfredspizzeria.com.au; 37 Barrack St; 3pm-midnight)

Cheeky Sparrow

BAR

21 MAP P36, C2

Cheeky Sparrow's multilevel floor of leather banquettes and bentwood chairs is great for everything from coffee to pizza, cheese and charcuterie plates. If you're feeling

Cocktails at Varnish on King

peckish later at night, pop in for robust bar snacks, including chorizo and lime, and chilli-cheese sliders. Cocktail fans certainly won't be disappointed. Access is via Wolf Lane – look out for the street art. (08-9486 4956; www.cheekysparrow.com.au; 1/317 Murray St; 3.30pm-late Tue-Thu, from noon Fri, from 3pm Sat)

Helvetica

BAR

22 MAP P36, C4

Clever arty types tap their toes to delicious alternative pop in this bar named after a typeface and specialising in whisky and cocktails. The concealed entry is off Howard St; look for the chandelier in the laneway and the street-art characters by internationally renowned local artist, Stormie Mills. (08-9321 4422; www.helveticabar.com.au; rear 101 St Georges Tce; 3-10pm Mon-Thu, noon-1am Fri, from 3pm Sat)

Hula Bula Bar

COCKTAIL BAR

23 MAP P36, G4

You'll feel like you're on *Gilligan's Island* in this tiny Polynesian-themed bar, decked out in bamboo, palm leaves and tikis. A cool but relaxed crowd jams in here on weekends to sip ostentatious cocktails out of ceramic monkey's heads. It's fun. (08-9225 4457; www.hulabulabar.com; 12 Victoria Ave; 4pm-midnight Tue-Thu, to 1am Fri, from 6pm Sat, noon-midnight Sun;)

Varnish on King

COCKTAIL BAR

24 MAP P36, C2

With edgy shopping, cafes and bars, lower King St shouldn't be

It's Just Not Cricket

Feared and respected by cricketers the world over, Perth's WACA (p47) Ground – the Western Australian Cricket Association's HQ on the edge of Central Perth – is famous for its rock-hard batting surfaces. Test cricket was first played here in the 1970–71 season, and for many decades, Australian fast-bowling firebrands like Dennis Lillee, Mitchell Johnson and Rodney Hogg sent down thunderbolts here, ricocheting off the hard turf and menacing hapless batsmen. The WACA pitch and outfield were *fast* – and beating Australia here took some serious doing. But now, the WACA's ageing infrastructure and the shifting tastes of Australia's cricket-watching public have spawned the Optus Stadium across the river. Will the flashy new arena, with its fancy lights and fireworks, become Australian cricket's new fortress? Will the pitch live up to the WACA tradition, or will spongy new 'drop-in' pitches change the way the cricketing world thinks about playing in Perth? Either way, for Perth's cricket fans, the times they are a-changin'.

overlooked. Amid the hipster barber shop and single-origin coffee is this brick-lined homage to American whiskey. More than 200 are available, best sampled with a bacon flight (yes, you read right). The open-late kitchen serves meaty yet refined fare. Think beef tendon chips with ash mayo. (☎08-9324 2237; www.varnishonking.com; 75 King St; ⏰11.30am-midnight Mon-Thu, to 2am Fri, from 4pm Sat)

Entertainment

Optus Stadium — STADIUM

25 ✪ MAP P36, H1

Perth's new 60,000-seat riverside stadium and its surrounding, family-friendly park (think playground, BBQs, sculptures) opened in January 2018. Big concerts, AFL games and international sport fixtures including cricket and rugby are held here. A new Perth Stadium train station services incoming crowds, while the Matagarup bridge links the stadium precinct with East Perth, enabling pedestrian access across the Swan River. (Perth Stadium; www.optusstadium.com.au; Victoria Park Dr, Burswood)

His Majesty's Theatre — THEATRE

26 ✪ MAP P36, B3

The majestic home to the West Australian Ballet (www.waballet.com.au) and West Australian Opera (www.waopera.asn.au), as well as lots of theatre, comedy and cabaret. (☎08-6212 9292; www.ptt.wa.gov.au/venues/his-majestys-theatre; 825 Hay St)

RAC Arena LIVE MUSIC

27 MAP P36, A1

Used for big concerts by major international acts such as Rhianna and the Rolling Stones, it's also used by the Perth Wildcats NBL basketball franchise and is home to West Coast Fever netball team. (Perth Arena; ☎08-6365 0700; www.pertharena.com.au; 700 Wellington St)

Amplifier LIVE MUSIC

28 MAP P36, B2

The good old Amplifier is one of the best places for live (mainly indie) bands. It's part of the same complex as Capitol, used mainly for DJ gigs. (☎08-9321 7606; www.amplifiercapitol.com.au; rear 383 Murray St)

Perth Concert Hall CONCERT VENUE

29 MAP P36, F5

Home to the Western Australian Symphony Orchestra (WASO; www.waso.com.au), this brutalist-style building also hosts big-name international acts, musicals and comedians. (☎08-9231 9999; www.perthconcerthall.com.au; 5 St Georges Tce)

WACA STADIUM

30 MAP P36, H5

Main venue for interstate and international cricket, and home to the Perth Scorchers domestic T20 team. Since 2018, one-day internationals have been held at Optus Stadium. (Western Australian Cricket Association; ☎08-9265 7222; www.waca.com.au; Nelson Cres)

Shopping

Boffins Books BOOKS

31 MAP P36, C3

Locally adored, Boffins' technical and specialist range includes travel. (☎08-9321 5755; www.boffinsbooks.com.au; 88 William St; 9am-5.30pm Mon-Thu, to 8pm-Fri, to 5pm Sat, noon-4pm Sun)

Worth a Trip

Swan Valley

Perth locals love to swan around this semirural vale on the city's northeastern suburban fringe. Any visit to the Swan Valley inevitably revolves around wine – there are more than 40 vineyards here, plus plenty of galleries, breweries, provedores and restaurants. Pick up a copy of the free Swan Valley Visitor Guide *and map from the visitor centre in Guildford, nominate someone else to drive and sip your way through the day.*

www.swanvalley.com.au

08-9207 8899

Swan Valley Wineries

Vines were first planted in the Swan Valley in the 1830s at Houghton winery, but it was after the arrival of Croatian settlers (from around 1916) that the farmland was increasingly transformed into a wine-production area. Perhaps in tacit acknowledgement that its wines will never compete with the state's more prestigious regions (it doesn't really have the ideal climate), the valley compensates by being as much a foodie destination as a wine region. Many of the wineries here have excellent built-in eating options, making it easy to lose track of time and ignore the desire to leave. A few of our faves:

RiverBank Estate (☎08-9377 1805; www.riverbankestate.com.au; 126 Hamersley Rd, Caversham; mains $29-65; ⏰cellar door 10am-4pm, lunch 11.30am-2.30pm) The pick of the region's winery restaurants, rustic RiverBank delivers excellent Mod Oz cuisine on its wrap-around veranda (or inside if it's hot). It's a little better dressed than the competition (hot tip: you too) and there's regular live jazz.

Sandalford Wines (☎08-9374 9374; www.sandalford.com; 3210 West Swan Rd, Caversham; tours $25, mains $35-45; ⏰10am-5pm, tours noon, restaurant noon-3pm) Sandalford is one of the oldest Swan Valley wineries (1840) and hosts high-society weddings and mainstream concerts on its expansive lawns. Sip some semillon at the cellar door, take a tour, or book a seat at the elegant restaurant for creative Mod Oz mains.

Houghton (☎08-9274 9540; www.houghton-wines.com.au; 148 Dale Rd, Middle Swan; ⏰10am-5pm) The Swan's oldest and best-known winery is surrounded by stroll-worthy grounds, including a jacaranda grove (check out the insanely purple blooms from late spring to early summer). Oh, and the wine's good too!

Pinelli Estate Wines (☎08-9377 7733; www.pinellirestaurant.com.au; 114 Benara Rd, Caversham;

★ Top Tips

- The **visitor centre** (Guildford Courthouse, cnr Swan & Meadow Sts; ⏰9am-4pm) is your first point of call for maps, brochures and advice.
- Bicycle touring is a possibility with **Perth Electrical Bike Hire** (☎0401 077 405; 1235 Great Northern Hwy, Upper Swan; standard/electric bikes per day $35/45), but the roads here are extremely busy.

✕ Take a Break

The **Rose & Crown** (☎08-9347 8100; www.rosecrown.com.au; 105 Swan St; mains breakfast $13-24, lunch & dinner $22-46; ⏰7am-late Mon-Fri, from 8am Sat & Sun) in Guildford is Western Australia's oldest still-operating pub.

★ Getting There

- Guildford falls within Zone 2 of Perth's public-transport system: catch a Midland line train from Perth Station.
- Myriad tour companies can deliver you here and show you around.

mains $18-42; ⌚11.30am-2.30pm Thu-Sun & 5.30pm-late Thu-Sat) Low-key and old school, Pinelli plates up authentic Italian risottos, pastas and meaty mains. Order a bottle of its summer-fresh chenin blanc and a plate of lamb-and-mushroom tortellini with pumpkin and braised beef cheek.

Guildford

It's part of Perth's suburban sprawl these days, but historically Guidford was a separate colony (founded 1829), and before that an important meeting hub for the local Wadjuk people. There's a cluster of interesting historic buildings here, and eating and drinking in Guildford is a pleasure, with some terrific old pubs and cafes on offer.

Various heritage walks start from the old **Guildford Courthouse** (☎08-9207 8899; www.swanguildfordhistoricalsociety.org.au; cnr Swan & Meadows Sts; admission free; ⌚9am-4pm); pick up the *Historic Guildford* map brochure from the Swan Valley Visitor Centre (inside the courthouse).

Swan Valley Craft Beer

Sure, the wine is great...but how about the beer!? A crop of outstanding craft-beer breweries has found a niche in the valley scene over recent years, offering a devilishly decent alternative to the grape. Our top picks:

Feral Brewing Company (☎08-9296 4657; www.feralbrewing.com.au; 152 Haddrill Rd, Baskerville; ⌚11am-5pm Sun-Thu, to late Fri &

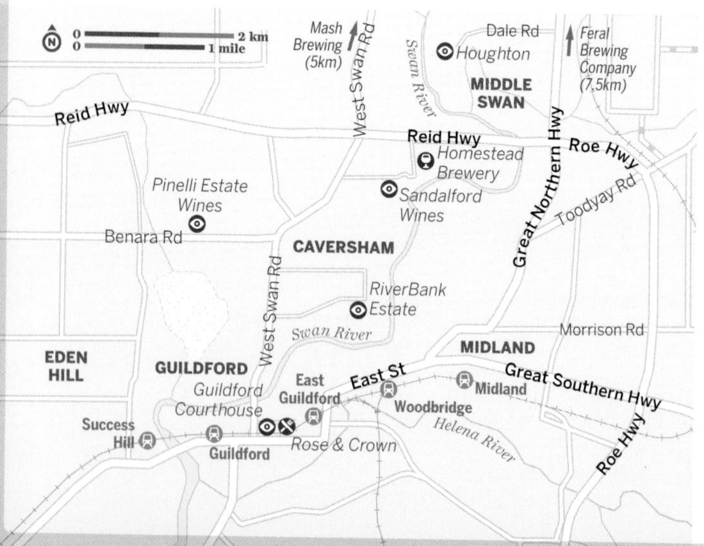

Local Hero

Guildford's most famous son was actor Heath Ledger, whose Hollywood star burned spectacularly until he died in 2008, aged just 28. Ledger was born in Perth and attended Guildford Grammar School, where he first cracked the boards as Peter Pan when he was 13. He got his Hollywood break in 1999 with *10 Things I Hate About You*. A string of successful starring roles followed, peaking with an Oscar-nominated performance as a gay cowboy in *Brokeback Mountain* in 2005, and a disquieting portrayal of the pathologically twisted Joker in the 2008 Batman flick *The Dark Knight*. Professionally Ledger was riding high, but he'd separated from actress Michelle Williams and was plagued by insomnia. He was found dead in his New York apartment on 22 January 2008, the subsequent autopsy concluding that he'd died from a lethal cocktail of anti-insomnia prescription drugs. In his honour, the main auditorium at the State Theatre Centre in Perth (p67) was named the 'Heath Ledger Theatre' when it opened in 2011.

Sat) Barrel-aged and sour brews, paired nicely with a robust pub-grub.

Homestead Brewery (☎ 08-6279 0500; www.mandoonestate.com.au/eat-drink/homestead-brewery; 10 Harris Rd, Caversham; ⏰10am-8.30pm Mon-Fri, 7.30am-10.30pm Sat & Sun) Standout brews include a zingy Bavarian wheat beer and an American pale ale. Food runs all day.

Mash Brewing (☎ 08-9296 5588; www.mashbrewing.com.au; 10250 West Swan Rd, Henley Brook; ⏰11am-5pm Sun-Thu, to 9pm Fri & Sat) Dude-filled Americana beer bunker pouring lager, ales, wheat beer and cider.

Guided Tours

Guided tours are a great way to see the valley, and not have to worry about driving home!

Out & About Wine Tours (☎ 08-9377 3376; www.outandabouttours.com.au; half-/full-day tours from $85/115) An experienced local operator running full-day, half-day and evening tours, including lunch and plenty of tastings. There's a river-cruise option too. Departs from Perth.

d'Vne Wine Tours (☎ 08-9244 5323; www.dvinetours.com.au; half-/full-day tours from $87/110) Good-humoured wine tours, either quick-fire or relaxed, with more good things to eat and drink than your body probably requires. Departs from Perth or Guildford.

Black Swan Tours (☎ 0458 771 734; www.blackswantours.com; half-/full-day tours from $69/105) Beer, wine, coffee, chocolate and cheese – small-group full- or half-day tours expose you to all of these. Departs from Perth or Guildford.

WINES OF WHILE
NATURAL WINE STORE + BAR
WESTONS
BARBERSHOP
&
SHAVE PARLOUR
WILLIAM TOPP

Explore

Northbridge

Just north of Central Perth, Northbridge crams a whole lotta fun into its compact grid of streets. This is where most of Perth's bars and clubs congregate, and (unsurprisingly) most of the city's backpacker hostels too. There are also some top places to eat here plus the Perth Cultural Centre: galleries, theatres, museums...

The Short List

- ***Art Gallery of Western Australia (p54)*** *Swooning before gorgeous canvases.*
- ***Drinking in Northbridge (p65)*** *Bouncing between bars, pubs and clubs.*
- ***Perth Institute of Contemporary Arts (p60)*** *Visiting PICA for contemporary art installations and performances.*
- ***Live music (p67)*** *Tuning in to some lilting jazz or cranking rock.*
- ***William St eats (p62)*** *Munching your way into budget Asian eats, some classy Greek tucker or a cafe breakfast.*

Getting There & Away

You can walk here from Central Perth in a matter of minutes: just head north (across a bridge!).

Jump on any bus from Central Perth (including the free blue CAT bus) heading north along William St.

Grab a cab from Central Perth to William St in Northbridge – a five- or 10-minute ride.

Neighbourhood Map on p58

Wines of While (p62), William St DOMONABIKE/ALAMY STOCK PHOTO ©

Top Sight

Art Gallery of Western Australia

Founded in 1895, this excellent gallery houses the state's pre-eminent art collection as well as regular international exhibitions, which, increasingly, have a modern, approachable bent. The permanent collection is arranged into wings, from contemporary to modern, and historic to local and Indigenous. Expect big-name Australian artists and diverse media including canvases, bark paintings and sculpture.

MAP P58, C6

08-9492 6622

www.artgallery.wa.gov.au

Perth Cultural Centre

admission free

10am-5pm Wed-Mon

It's Nice in Here

Wandering slowly through Art Gallery of Western Australia is a peaceful way to get to know the state's creative and historical sides. The vast ceilings and airy spaces leave plenty of room for pop art sculptures, painted Aboriginal poles, bush scenes lit by Australia's magical light and photography that stops you in your tracks. You could focus on the big names – Arthur Boyd, Russell Drysdale, Sidney Nolan, Frederick McCubbin – and see it all in an hour, or give yourself half a day to really explore: either way you'll feel rewarded as you step back out into the city sunshine.

Galleries, Tours & Talks

Volunteers run free **guided tours** of the gallery – a great way to give some context to the good stuff on the walls. Tours cover various themes and eras: historical, modern, contemporary and Western Australian, reflecting the content of the various gallery spaces here. The contemporary collection is particularly engaging, extending its remit beyond painted canvases to embrace sound, film, craft and design. Most works are displayed within the main building, a cream-coloured brutalist concrete structure that opened in 1979 (love it or hate it – the building tends to polarise architectural opinions), with the historical collection housed in the old court house galleries off to one side.

Tours leave at 1pm every day (except Tuesday), with extra 11am tours on Mondays and Wednesdays. There are also quick-fire 'Art Snacks' **lunchtime tours** on Wednesdays (12.30pm) and Thursdays (noon). No need to book – just turn up. Tours of **visiting exhibitions** and **artists' talks** also transpire. The schedule does tend to shift around from time to time: have a look at www.artgallery.wa.gov.au/discover/gallery-guides to confirm what's on.

★ Top Tips

- Don't miss *Down on His Luck* by Frederick McCubbin (1889), an Australian classic depicting a mournful swagman; and Hans Heysen's 1921 *Droving Into the Light*, which is almost as iconic.
- Myriad Aboriginal works include the crowd-pleasing *Kimberley Landscape* by Paddy Jaminji and *Funeral Ceremony* by Mawalan Marika.
- On hot days, this is the air-conditioned place to be. On cold days, bring a cardigan.
- The Imagination Room is tailored to children and families, with plenty of free stuff.
- Selfie sticks are deeply un-arty – don't even think about it.

✕ Take a Break

- The gallery cafe, **Frank Express** (www.artgallery.wa.gov.au/plan-your-visit/eat-drink) serves coffee, fancy sandwiches and bowl food (awesome pumpkin soup).

Walking Tour

Northbridge Bar Crawl

Hankering for a drink? Of course you are! There's no better place in Perth than Northbridge for a little quenching. Many of the bars along William St are big, brawly beer barns without a whole lot of soul, but this bar crawl takes you to six of the neighbourhood's quirkier, local-secret booze rooms. Give yourself half an hour in each.

Walk Facts

Start Alabama Song; Perth Station

End Northbridge Brewing Company; Perth Station

Length 1km; three hours

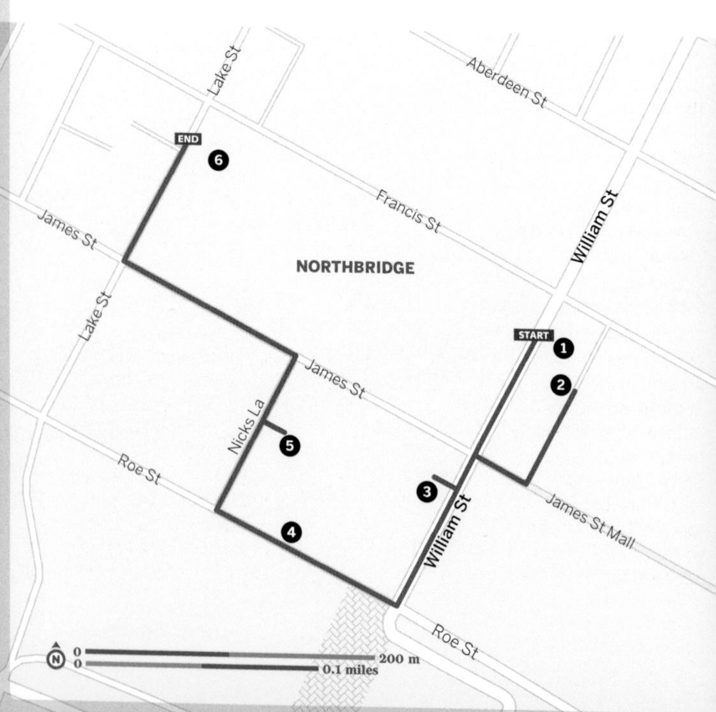

❶ Alabama Song

Kick-start your crawl with a dose of the Deep South. One of Northbridge's best back-alley bars – compact, bespoke and offbeat – Alabama Song (p65) is adorned with Americana, and bar staff pouring a dizzying array of whiskeys and bourbons. Rye paradise! Like Jim Morrison, you might need someone to show you the way to the next whisky bar, off a James St laneway.

❷ Mechanics Institute

Turn left off William St into James St, then take the sneaky alley behind the Alex Hotel to discover the Mechanics Institute (p65), a bricky bar at roof level. Discuss the absence of mechanics and possessive apostrophes over a WA craft beer and burger, then head downstairs and back into the William St fray.

❸ Ezra Pound

The fantastically named Ezra Weston Loomis Pound was an expat American 20th-century poet of dubious political affiliation. Discuss Mussolini, stanzas and iambic pentameter over a barrel-aged Black Manhattan at his intimate namesake bar (p66), down a narrow graffiti-spangled laneway to your right (off William St). Great bar food too, if you're peckish.

❹ The Standard

Around the corner on Roe St, the Standard (p65) is a far-above-standard bar that's as good for a few adventurous Mod Oz share plates as it is for a late-night negroni or a Western Australian Eagle Bay Black IPA. Order some caramelised kangaroo with sesame soy, pineapple and lime and see where the conversation takes you. The standard has been raised.

❺ Sneaky Tony's

To sneak into Sneaky Tony's (p65), a secretive little bar around the corner in Chinatown off Nicks Lane, you'll need the secret password (try 'Open Sesame'...or check Facebook). The vibe is candlelit and woody, with attentive barkeeps who really know their stuff. It's arguably Perth's best bar (oh how they argue), but don't linger: your final stop awaits.

❻ Northbridge Brewing Company

Head north towards James St, turn left and pass a couple of Perth's better clubs (Geisha and Air), then turn right onto Lake St until you hit Northbridge Brewing Company (p66). After all those cocktails, it's time for a cleansing ale: prop yourself at the bar adjoining grassy Northbridge Plaza and sip a frosty Beerland Kolsch. Call it a night?

0 200 m
0 0.1 miles

For reviews see

Top Sights	p54
Sights	p60
Eating	p62
Drinking	p65
Entertainment	p67
Shopping	p69

A B C D

1 2 3 4 5 6

Brisbane St
Robinson Ave
William St
6
34
Forbes Rd
Lake St
Perth Steam Works
5
Forbes Rd
Newcastle St
4
Graham Farmer Fwy (Northbridge Tunnel)
12
Lt Parry St
Russell Sq
Parker St
Aberdeen St
29
Money St
Newcastle St
Francis St
Lake St
11
21
8
1 Nostalgia Box
32
14
Aberdeen St
NORTHBRIDGE
William St
James St
Lake St
19
18
30
Francis St
Perth Cultural Centre
Nick's La
26
16
25
Western Australian Museum – Perth
Roe St
17
23
9
20
Beaufort St
13
7
James St Mall
22
2
3
15
28
Perth Institute of Contemporary Arts
24
Art Gallery of Western Australia
Roe St
Horseshoe Bridge
Queen St
William St
Wellington St
Perth
Beaufort St

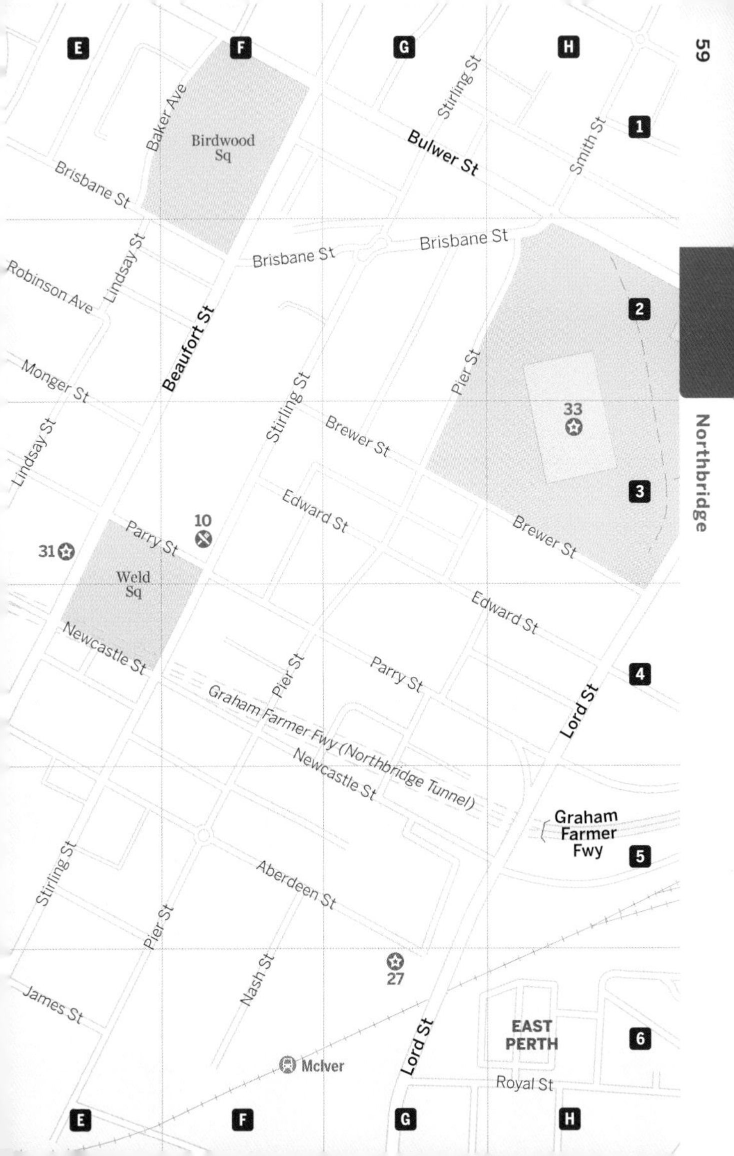

E
F
G
H
Stirling St
1
Baker Ave
Birdwood Sq
Bulwer St
Smith St
Brisbane St
Brisbane St
Brisbane St
Lindsay St
Robinson Ave
2
Beaufort St
Monger St
Pier St
Stirling St
33
Brewer St
Lindsay St
3
Edward St
Brewer St
10
Parry St
31
Weld Sq
Edward St
Newcastle St
Pier St
Parry St
4
Graham Farmer Fwy (Northbridge Tunnel)
Lord St
Newcastle St
Graham Farmer Fwy
5
Stirling St
Aberdeen St
Pier St
Nash St
27
James St
Lord St
EAST PERTH
6
McIver
Royal St
E
F
G
H

Sights

Nostalgia Box

MUSEUM

1 MAP P58, D4

Ease into poignant, low-pixel childhood memories of Atari, Nintendo and Super Mario at this surprisingly interesting collection of retro 1970s and '80s gaming consoles and arcade games. Along the way you'll learn about the history of gaming, and there are plenty of consoles to jump onto and see if the old skills are still there from a few decades back. (08-9227 7377; www.thenostalgiabox.com.au; 16 Aberdeen St; adult/child/family $17/12/50; 11am-4pm Sun-Mon & Wed-Fri, to 5pm Sat;)

Perth Institute of Contemporary Arts

GALLERY

2 MAP P58, C5

PICA (*pee*-kah) may look traditional – it's housed in an elegant 1896 red-brick former school – but inside it's one of Australia's principal platforms for contemporary art, including installations, performance, sculpture and video. PICA actively promotes new and experimental art, and it exhibits graduate works annually. From 10am to late, Tuesday to Sunday, the **PICA Bar** is a top spot for a coffee or cocktail, and has occasional live music. (08-9228 6300; www.pica.org.au; Perth Cultural Centre; admission free; 10am-5pm Tue-Sun)

Western Australian Museum – Perth

MUSEUM

3 MAP P58, D5

The state's museum is a six-headed beast, with branches in Albany, Geraldton and Kalgoorlie as well as two in Fremantle. This main branch in Northbridge is closed for renovations and is due to reopen as the renamed New Museum for Western Australia in 2020. See online for an outline of the project. While the hub is closed, key exhibits are being displayed as pop-ups

New Museum for Western Australia

The **Western Australian Museum – Perth** in Northbridge was already an impressive institution when it closed in 2016 to undergo a four-year renovation. More than $400 million later, the 2020 reopening of the rebranded **New Museum for Western Australia** is set to be nothing short of spectacular! Morphing out of the museum's existing red-brick heritage buildings like some kind of architectural alien, the low-emissions New Museum will feature 6000 sq metres of gallery space, including a dedicated 1000-sq-metre space for large-scale exhibitions. At the time of writing, building works were on track: watch this space.

Perth Institute of Contemporary Arts (PICA)

at other venues around town – see the website for details.

One of the Northbridge location's most interesting exhibits is currently on loan to the Maritime Museum (p124) in Fremantle. Set in its own preservative bath, Megamouth is a curious-looking species of shark with a soft, rounded head. Only about five of these benign creatures have ever been found; this one beached itself near Mandurah, south of Perth. (☎08-6552 7800; www.museum.wa.gov.au; Perth Cultural Centre; admission free; ⏰9.30am-5pm)

Rockface CLIMBING

4 ◉ MAP P58, A2

Inside an old brick warehouse abutting the Mitchell Fwy, Rockface has an impressive array of indoor climbing walls, bouldering areas, slabs and overhangs. Don your nifty rubber shoes, clip your rope to your harness and up you go. Good fun for kids too. (☎08-9328 5998; www.rockface.com.au; 63b John St; climbing with/without gear hire adult $30/20, child $27/17; ⏰10am-10pm Mon-Fri, 9am-6pm Sat & Sun; 👪)

Perth Steam Works BATHHOUSE

5 ◉ MAP P58, D2

Gay men's sauna, with an on-site bar and cafe. The entry is on Forbes St. (☎08-9328 2930; www.perthsteamworks.com.au; 369 William St; $25; ⏰noon-1am Sun-Thu, to 2am Fri & Sat)

Eating

Wines of While

AUSTRALIAN $

6 MAP P58, D1

A 50-seater wine bar that's fast become known for its great value and incredibly flavoursome food. Surprisingly, the bar's run by a young, qualified doctor who still works as a surgical assistant on Mondays. His true passion is natural wine, but he's a phenomenal cook. Get the ricotta-zucchini salad, the house-baked bread and zesty lemon white beans. (08-9328 3332; www.winesofwhile.com; 458 William St; mains $10-24; noon-midnight Tue-Sat, to 10pm Sun)

Bivouac Canteen & Bar

CAFE $$

7 MAP P58, B5

Flavour-jammed, Middle Eastern–influenced cuisine partners with a good wine list, craft beers and artisanal ciders. Always-busy Bivouac's white walls are adorned with a rotating roster of work from local artists. The lamb ribs in a lemon glaze are a great way to kick off the meal, followed by the Palestinian-style nine-spice chicken. (08-9227 0883; www.bivouac.com.au; 198 William St; small plates $9-19, large plates $28-34; noon-late Tue-Sat)

Little Willys

CAFE $

8 MAP P58, C4

The name here pertains to the cafe's petite size, and the fact it sits on William St – don't get any funny ideas. Grab a footpath table and tuck into robust treats such as the city's best breakfast burrito and Bircher muesli. It's also a preferred coffee haunt for the hip Northbridge indie set. BYO skinny jeans. (08-9228 8240; 267 William St; mains $10-19; 6am-4pm Mon-Fri, from 8am Sat & Sun)

Sauma

INDIAN $$

9 MAP P58, B5

Punchy Indian street-food flavours feature at this corner location in Northbridge that always has the windows open wide. Interesting antiques surround the main bar dispensing Indian-inspired cocktails and Swan Valley beers, while the shared tables are crowded with diners tucking into chai-smoked oysters, chargrilled chilli-squid salad and a terrific, rustic goat curry. (08-9227 8682; www.sauma.com.au; 200 William St; mains $16-29; 5-10pm Tue & Wed, 11am-10.30pm Thu & Sun, to 11pm Fri & Sat)

Brika

GREEK $$

10 MAP P58, F3

Presenting a stylish spin on rustic Greek cuisine, off the main drag Brika is a load of fun. The white-washed interior is enlivened by colourful traditional fabrics. Menu highlights include creamy smoked-eggplant dip, slow-cooked lamb and charred calamari. Definitely leave room for a dessert of *loukoumades* (Greek doughnuts).

Perth Street Art

Take a walk around the Perth suburbs – Northbridge is a prime example – and on any empty span of wall you'll most likely spy a fabulous mural. The city has seen a boom in street-art culture in recent years – not just off-the-cuff tags and quick graffiti jobs, but gorgeously imaginative, creative pieces by established local and international mural artists. Cafes and bars in particular are clamouring to commission a bit of colour, aided by sympathetic local councils and the police, who tend to turn a blind eye to illegal, uncommissioned pieces these days. For the low-down on the Perth street-art scene, with loads of photographs, an interactive map and links to Facebook pages for individual suburbs, check out www.streetsofperthwa.com.

If you're pushed for time, grab an espresso, baklava and a souvlaki wrap from Brika's Filos + Yiros hole-in-the-wall option (open 7.30am to 4pm daily). There's a pleasant park just across the road to sit while you eat. (0455 321 321; www.brika.com.au; 3/177 Stirling St; meze & mains $12-35; 5pm-late Mon-Thu, from noon Fri-Sun)

Henry Summer AUSTRALIAN $$

11 MAP P58, C3

The size of a pub with the feel of a small bar, Henry Summer woos with cascading plants and fronded canopies, open-air spaces and a welcoming vibe. The menu blends premixed cocktails with wood-fired meats and raw salads. Collect your dishes from a pink neon sign declaring 'Pick up spot' and see what – or who – else you encounter. (www.lavishhabits.com.au/venues/henry-summer; 69 Aberdeen St; noon-midnight Sun-Thu, to 2am Fri & Sat; ; free CAT)

Tak Chee House MALAYSIAN $

12 MAP P58, D3

With Malaysian students crammed in for a taste of home, Tak Chee is one of the best Asian cheapies along William St. If you don't have a taste for satay, Hainan chicken or *char kway teo* (fried noodles), Thai, Vietnamese, Lao and Chinese flavours are all just footsteps away. Cash only; BYO wine or beer. (08-9328 9445; 1/364 William St; mains $11-18; 11am-9pm Tue-Sun)

Kakulas Bros DELI $

13 MAP P58, B5

A local institution since 1929, this fragrant provisions store overflows with sacks and vats of legumes, nuts, dried fruits and olives, plus a deli counter that's well stocked with cheese and meats. The coffee beans are roasted on-site. There's another branch, Kakulas Sister (p137), in Fremantle. (☎08-9328 5285; www.kakulasbros.com.au; 183 William St; ⏰8am-5pm Mon-Sat, 11am-4pm Sun; 🖊)

Hummus Club

MIDDLE EASTERN $$

14 MAP P58, C4

If you can nab a seat on the open-air balcony, consider yourself lucky. Hummus Club has become one of Northbridge's coolest foodie haunts, not least for its creamy hummus served with spiced beef and toasted almonds, lamb kofta, falafel and watermelon fattoush salad. Cocktails using local craft spirits and Lebanese Almaza beer complement a fun vibe. (☎08-9227 8215; www.thehummusclub.com; 258 William St; mains $14-18; ⏰5-10pm Tue-Thu & Sun, from noon Fri & Sat; 🖊)

Chicho Gelato

GELATO $

15 MAP P58, B5

Hands down Perth's best gelato. With innovative flavours like avocado with candied bacon, and everything made from real ingredients (no fake flavourings here), it's easy to see why. Expect queues in the evening – don't worry, the line moves quickly – and ask about current collaborations with local chefs. Do pay $1 extra to have melted chocolate poured into your waffle cone. (www.chichogelato.com; 180 William St; from $5; ⏰noon-10pm Sun-Wed, to 11pm Thu-Sat)

Chicho Gelato

Drinking

Sneaky Tony's

BAR

16 MAP P58, B5

On Friday and Saturday you'll need the password to enter this speakeasy amid street art and Chinese restaurants – don't worry, it's revealed weekly on Sneaky Tony's Facebook page. Once inside, park yourself at the long bar and order a rum cocktail. Try the refreshing Dark & Stormy with ginger beer and lime. The hidden entrance is behind 28 Roe St. (www.facebook.com/sneakytonys; Nicks Lane; 4pm-midnight)

The Standard

BAR

17 MAP P58, B5

Effortlessly straddling the divide between bar and restaurant, the Standard carries Northbridge's arty vibe into its colourful interior. Head through to the summery, courtyard garden and its shipping-container deck for the most raffish ambience, and partake in a Pimm's or spritz and such playful share plates as KFC cauliflower and toasted-coconut ceviche. (08-9228 1331; www.thestandardperth.com.au; 28 Roe St; 4pm-midnight Mon-Thu, from noon Fri & Sat, to 10pm Sun)

Mechanics Institute

BAR

18 MAP P58, C4

Negotiate the laneway entrance via the James St cul-de-sac – behind Alex Hotel – to discover one of Perth's most easy-going rooftop bars. Share one of the big, pine tables on the deck or nab a bar stool. Brilliant cocktails are readily shaken, craft beers are on tap, and you can even order in a gourmet burger from sister venue, **Flipside** (08-9228 8822; www.flipsideburgerbar.com.au; burgers $8-15; 11.30am-9.30pm Mon-Wed, to late Thu-Sat, noon-9pm Sun), downstairs. (08-9228 4189; www.mechanicsinstitutebar.com.au; 222 William St; noon-midnight Mon-Sat, to 10pm Sun)

Alabama Song

BAR

19 MAP P58, C4

Featuring over 130 rye whiskies and bourbons, Alabama Song is a fun, late-night dive bar down a back lane in Northbridge. Chicken wings and cheeseburgers are impressively good, and on Friday and Saturday nights live bands and DJs rip through rockabilly, honky tonk and country classics. Don't forget your John Deere trucker cap, worn with a side of irony. (www.facebook.com/alabamasongbar; level 1, behind 232 William St; 6pm-2am Wed-Sat, from 8pm Sun)

LOT 20

BAR

20 MAP P58, C5

LOT 20 is evidence of the transformation of rough-and-ready Northbridge into the home of more intimate and sophisticated small bars. The brick-lined courtyard is perfect on a warm WA evening, and on cooler nights the cosy interior is best experienced with bar snacks, gourmet burgers and WA wine or Aussie craft beer. The entrance is via the James St cul-de-sac. (☎08-6162 1195; www.lot20.co; 198-206 William St; ⏲10am-midnight Sun-Tue, from noon Wed-Sat)

Northbridge Brewing Company

MICROBREWERY

21 MAP P58, A4

The beers brewed here are decent enough, but the real attractions are the occasional on-tap guest beers from around Australia. The outdoor bar adjoining the grassy expanse of Northbridge Plaza is relaxed and easy-going, and various big screens dotted around the multilevel industrial space make this a good spot to watch live sport. (☎08-6151 6481; www.northbridgebrewingco.com.au; 44 Lake St; ⏲11am-late Sun-Thu, to 2am Fri & Sat)

Bird

BAR

22 MAP P58, B5

A cool indie bar lined with wood and bird cages, leading to a stage regularly ruled by local bands, performers and DJs. One of Perth's few live-music venues, it has an excellent brick courtyard out the back, filled with dog-eared couches and chatterboxes. (www.williamstreetbird.com; 181 William St; ⏲11.30am-midnight Mon-Sat, to 11pm Sun)

Ezra Pound

BAR

23 MAP P58, B5

Down a much-graffitied laneway leading off William St, Ezra Pound is favoured by Northbridge's tattooed, arty, bohemian set. It's the kind of place where you can settle into a red-velvet chair and sip a Tom Collins out of a jam jar. Earnest conversations about Kerouac and Kafka are strictly optional. (☎0401 347 471; www.ezrapound.com.au; 189 William St; ⏲3pm-midnight Mon-Thu, from 1pm Fri & Sat, to 10pm Sun)

The Court

BAR

24 MAP P58, D5

A large, rambling complex consisting of an old corner pub and a big, partly covered courtyard with a clubby atmosphere, jamming in six bars and three dance floors. Wednesday is drag night, with kings and queens holding court in front of a young crowd. All sexual persuasions welcome. (☎08-9328 5292; www.thecourt.com.au; 50 Beaufort St; ⏲noon-10pm Sun-Tue, to midnight Wed-Thu, to 2am Fri & Sat)

Connections

CLUB

25 MAP P58, B5

DJs, drag shows and the occasional bit of lesbian mud wrestling. The rooftop bar space is great if you need to come up for (fresh) air. (☎08-9328 1870; www.connectionsnightclub.com; 81 James St; ⏲8pm-late Wed-Sat)

Drinking in Northbridge

Let's cut to the chase: we all know why you're here. Northbridge after dark is about as much fun as you can have with your clothes on (and sometimes without). Yes, the bar scene here can get messy, but it's easy enough to sidestep the craziness if you're not in the mood. There are more than enough hip little cocktail bars and live-music haunts to keep you out of trouble. We hate to sound prudish, but sidestep the Saturday-night crowds here if you want your Northbridge experience to retain a modicum of decorum (or dive right in if you don't); Friday evenings are far more fun. William St is the main thoroughfare, but you'll also find some cool bars along James St, Roe St and on Beaufort St. Strung along William St north of Newcastle St is a collection of great Asian restaurants – the perfect place to counterbalance your after-dark libations with some carbohydrates. For a detailed look at William St's offerings, check out www.onwilliam.com.au.

Entertainment

Rooftop Movies

CINEMA

26 MAP P58, A5

Art-house, classic movies and new releases screen under the stars on the 6th floor of a Northbridge car park. Beanbags, wood-fired pizza and craft beer all combine for a great night out. Booking ahead online is recommended and don't be surprised if you're distracted from the on-screen action by the city views. Score $14 tickets on cheap Tuesdays. (08-9227 6288; www.rooftopmovies.com.au; 68 Roe St; online/door $16/17; Tue-Sun late Oct-late Mar)

Badlands Bar

LIVE MUSIC

27  MAP P58, G6

Located on the fringes of Northbridge, Badlands has shrugged off its previous incarnation as a retro 1950s-inspired nightclub to be reborn as an edgy rock venue. The best WA bands are regulars, and if an up-and-coming international band is touring, Badlands is the place to see them before they become really famous. Check online for listings. (0498 239 273; www.badlands.bar; 3 Aberdeen St; 6pm-2am Fri & Sat)

State Theatre Centre

THEATRE

28 MAP P58, B5

This stunning complex filled with gold tubes hanging from the ceil-

Nullifying the Night

As per Kings Cross in Sydney, Fortitude Valley in Brisbane and Hindley St in Adelaide, things can get ugly in Northbridge in the wee small hours. After a spate of violent late-night incidents in Sydney, including several deaths, in 2014 the New South Wales state government introduced 'lock-out' laws, requiring pubs, bars and clubs to lock their doors to new arrivals at 1.30am and call last drinks at 3am.

Yes, the rates of booze-fuelled violence declined, but at the considerable cost to the live-music scene, the small-business economy and the sense that Sydney had any sort of pulse after midnight. Queensland introduced similar laws in 2016, and it looked like Perth would follow suit after an all-in Northbridge street brawl in May of the same year and a third of Perth's hospital beds being taken up by damaged drunks on weekends. But, bolstered by stats suggesting a 36% downturn in street violence since 2008, and perhaps fearing the impact of such laws on an already cooling WA economy, the state government decided to stick with the status quo (3.30am last entry, 5am last drinks).

So enjoy your predawn drinks in Northbridge this Saturday night – but don't go throwing any chairs through windows and starting a ruckus now, y'hear?

ing includes the 575-seat Heath Ledger Theatre and the 234-seat Studio Underground. It hosts performances by the Black Swan State Theatre Company, Yirra Yaakin Theatre Company and the Barking Gecko young people's theatre. Serious, challenging and deeply artistic performances are regularly held. (☎08-6212 9292; www.ptt.wa.gov.au/venues/state-theatre-centre-of-wa; 174 William St)

Moon
LIVE MUSIC

29 MAP P58, C3

A low-key, late-night cafe that's been running for more than 20 years and is regarded as a local institution, particularly by students. It has singer-songwriters on Wednesday night, jazz on Thursday and poetry slams on Saturday afternoon from 2pm. (☎08-9328 7474; www.themoon.com.au; 323 William St; 5pm-1am Mon-Thu, noon-late Fri-Sun)

Universal
LIVE MUSIC

30 MAP P58, B4

The unpretentious Universal is one of Perth's oldest live-music bars and much loved by soul, R&B and blues enthusiasts. All ages hit their groove on the dance floor. It ain't pretty, but it is fun. (08-9227 6771; www.universalbar.com.au; 221 William St; 3pm-1am Wed-Thu, 11.30am-2am Fri, from 4pm Sat, to midnight Sun)

Ellington Jazz Club

JAZZ

31 MAP P58, E3

There's live jazz nightly in this handsome, intimate venue staging professional-level jazz in all its forms. Standing-only admission is $10, or you can book a table ($15 to $20 per person) for tapas and pizza. (08-9228 1088; www.ellingtonjazz.com.au; 191 Beaufort St; 6.30-10pm Mon-Thu, to 1.30am Fri & Sat, 5.30-9pm Sun)

Cinema Paradiso

CINEMA

32 MAP P58, A4

Art-house, independent and foreign movies are shown at this cinema in the heart of Northbridge. (08-6559 0490; www.palacecinemas.com.au/cinemas/cinema-paradiso; 164 James St)

HBF Park

STADIUM

33 MAP P58, H3

Home to Perth Glory soccer (football) and Western Force rugby clubs. (Perth Oval; 08-9422 1500; www.hbfpark.com.au; 310 Pier St)

Shopping

William Topp

DESIGN

34 MAP P58, D1

Cool designer knick-knacks, one-off finds, handmade ceramics and framed tea towels: if you need a quirky gift, this is your spot. (08-9228 8733; www.williamtopp.com; 452 William St; 10.30am-5.30pm Mon-Fri, 10am-5pm Sat, 11am-4pm Sun)

Explore

Highgate & Mount Lawley

Two of Perth's more lovely residential neighbourhoods, Highgate and adjoining Mount Lawley extend northeast from Northbridge along Beaufort St. This is a land of photogenic Federation-era houses on quiet tree-lined streets—and if you're at all interested in cafes, bakeries, sassy wine bars and multicultural restaurants, this is your happy place.

The Short List

- ***Cafe & bakeries (p75)*** *Ordering a short black or slice of sourdough.*
- ***Hyde Park (p78)*** *Snoozing under a Moreton Bay fig or chasing the kids through the fountains.*
- ***Wine bars & pubs (p78)*** *Welcoming the evening in stylish bars and music haunts.*
- ***Astor (p80)*** *Catching some comedy, live music or an art-house flick.*
- ***Beaufort St shops (p81)*** *Browsing through eclectic small shops and boutiques.*

Getting There & Around

Buses cruise up Beaufort St from Central Perth: jump on bus 66, 67, 68 or 950.

Urban-hike your way up Beaufort St from the city through Highgate and into Mount Lawley.

This part of Perth is serviced by East Perth (for Highgate) and Mount Lawley train stations, both on the Midland line from Perth Station.

Neighbourhood Map on p74

Hyde Park (p75)

Walking Tour

Beaufort Street Shuffle

Get a feel for Highgate's beautiful parks and the cafes and booze-rooms along Mount Lawley's Beaufort St strip on this easy-going neighbourhood stroll. The walk will take you off the main drag then back onto it, just in time for your meal or beverage of choice.

Walk Facts

Start Birdwood Sq; East Perth Station

End Astor; Mt Lawley Station

Length 3.5km; one hour

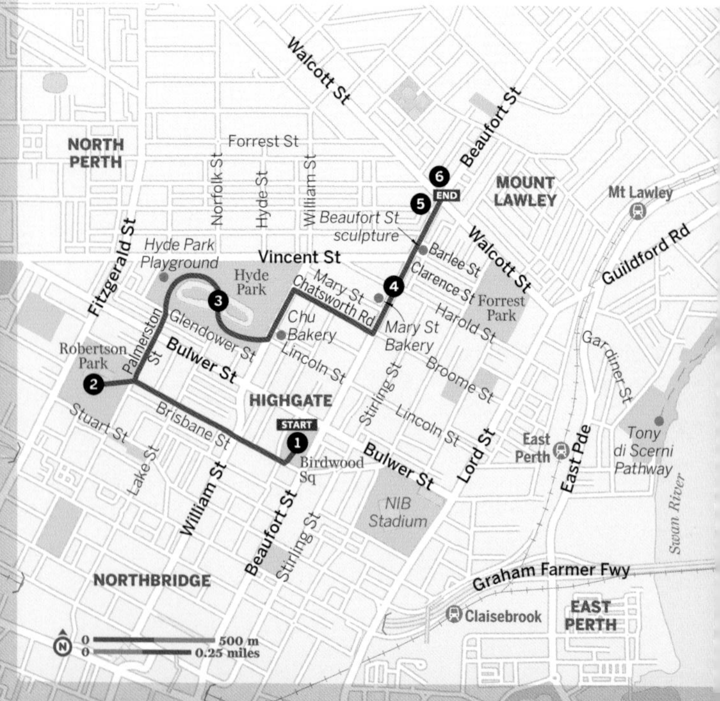

❶ Birdwood Square

On the quiet lower reaches of Beaufort St, **Birdwood Sq** is one of many green zones around this part of Perth. It's just across the road from a sociable backpackers, so there are usually a few Frisbees flying and hangovers receding here.

❷ Robertson Park

Head west along Brisbane St into low-key Highgate, towards **Robertson Park**, home to a complex of grass tennis courts and some of the biggest Moreton Bay fig trees you'll ever eyeball.

❸ Hyde Park

Track north on Palmerston St to expansive Hyde Park (p75), originally a wetland known as Boodjamooling to the Wadjuk. The 'Hyde Park' moniker was adopted in 1899 after 'Third Swamp' was deemed to lack a certain appeal. The excellent Hyde Park Playground (excellent if you're a kid) occupies the high terrain to the left. Arc around the twin lakes and deposit yourself on William St: Chu Bakery (p77) and its killer doughnuts await you.

❹ Beaufort Street

Head east on Lincoln St, turn north on Cavendish St then right onto Chatsworth Rd until you hit **Beaufort St**, Highgate and Mount Lawley's main thoroughfare. Head north in search of cafes, bakeries and bars (you won't have to go too far). Mary Street Bakery (p77) is hard to beat for a coffee, a slab of cake or even a beer.

❺ Flying Scotsman

Beyond Vincent St, check out the artfully rendered Beaufort St sculpture on the right just south of Barlee St. Further north, more drinking dens, shops and cafes cluster around the broad intersection of Beaufort and Walcott Sts, including the 1934-built Flying Scotsman (p79). A subversive dose of indie spirit amid Mount Lawley's more formal protocols, it's a super spot for a drink.

❻ Astor

Cross Walcott St and see who's playing at the Astor (p80), one of Perth's best midsized music venues. Stand-up comedy also gets a run here, as do occasional art-house films and spoken-word events. Enjoy!

Escape to the River

Beaufort St can feel a bit too urban and hectic at times: it's easy to forget that this part of Perth actually fronts onto the Swan River. Take some time out down by the water at **Banks Reserve** (off Gardiner St, beyond the rail lines) and the lovely **Tony di Scerni Pathway**, which winds upstream from Banks Reserve along the riverbank.

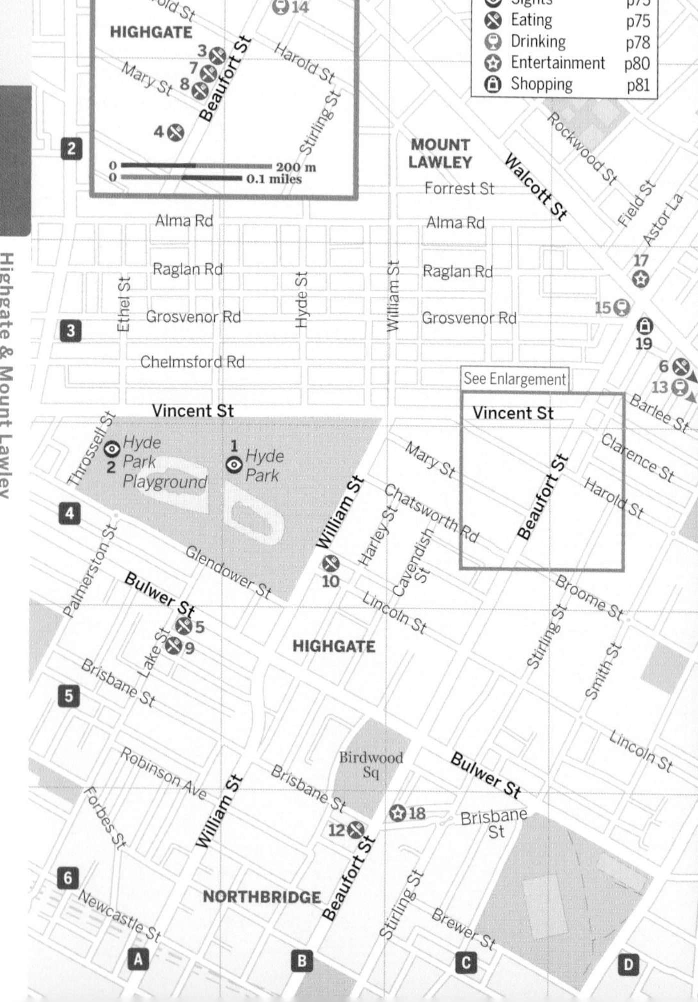

For reviews see
Sights p75
Eating p75
Drinking p78
Entertainment p80
Shopping p81
400 m
0.2 miles
200 m
0.1 miles
See Enlargement
HIGHGATE
MOUNT LAWLEY
NORTHBRIDGE
Vincent St
Harold St
Mary St
Beaufort St
Stirling St
Rockwood St
Walcott St
Field St
Astor La
Forrest St
Alma Rd
Raglan Rd
Grosvenor Rd
Chelmsford Rd
Ethel St
Hyde St
William St
Barlee St
Clarence St
Throssell St
Hyde Park Playground
Hyde Park
Chatsworth Rd
Harley St
Cavendish St
Palmerston St
Glendower St
Bulwer St
Lake St
Lincoln St
Broome St
Smith St
Brisbane St
Robinson Ave
Forbes St
Birdwood Sq
Newcastle St
Brewer St

Sights

Hyde Park

PARK

1 MAP P74, B4

One of Perth's most beautiful parks, suburban Hyde Park is a top spot for a picnic or lazy book-reading session on the lawn, as fountains flow. A path traces a split lake, and sprawling Moreton Bay figs provide plenty of shade. Kids love the playground and free water park. It's within walking distance of Northbridge; continue northeast along William St. (William St, Highgate;)

Hyde Park Playground

PLAYGROUND

2 MAP P74, A4

Highgate's reverently named Hyde Park may not have its London namesake's grandeur, but it does have a fabulous water park (squirting jets, happy kids), a big playground, open lawns, ice-cream trucks and a lake with turtles in it. If the kids can't find something here to keep them entertained, we give up. (08-9273 6000; www.vincent.wa.gov.au/parks-and-facilities/item/hyde-park; Throssell St, Highgate; admission free; daylight hours;)

Eating

Must Winebar

FRENCH **$$$**

3 MAP P74, A1

One of Perth's best wine bars, Must is also one of the city's slickest restaurants with a cheeky, playful vibe that particularly resonates on Fridays, when Champagne and shucked oysters flow. The menu marries smart modern-Australian numbers with excellent local produce. A French-bistro influence wafts through, particularly in the bar snacks; the house charcuterie plate is legendary. (08-9328 8255; www.must.com.au; 519 Beaufort St, Highgate; bar snacks $6-23, mains $23-38; 4pm-midnight Tue-Thu & Sat, from noon Fri)

St Michael 6003

MODERN AUSTRALIAN **$$$**

4 MAP P74, A2

Welcome to one of the city's classiest and most elegant restaurants. Like so many of Perth's eateries, the emphasis here is on smaller shared plates, but there's some serious culinary wizardry in the kitchen. Menu highlights could include locally sourced marron (freshwater lobster), scallops, quail and lamb. Sign up for the seven-course menu ($95 per person) for a leisurely treat. (08-9328 1177; www.stmichael6003.com.au; 483 Beaufort St, Highgate; starters $18-21, mains $28-39; 6-10pm Tue-Sat & noon-3pm Fri)

Sayers Sister

CAFE **$$**

5 MAP P74, A5

Top-notch brunch options – including leek and Parmesan croquettes in dreamy leek cream with poached eggs – combine with eclectic interiors that are said to be inspired by the long-time owners' home. Plonk down in an armchair or perch on the bench table for fine-quality, seasonal fare a short walk from leafy Hyde Park. Breakfast cocktails add to the fun. (08-9227 7506; www.sayerssister.com.au; 236 Lake St, Highgate; mains $14-28; 7am-4pm Mon-Fri, to 3pm Sat & Sun)

Mrs S

CAFE $$

6 MAP P74, D3

Mrs S has a quirky retro ambience, the perfect backdrop for beautifully decorated cakes, a healthy breakfast or a lazy brunch. Menus – presented in Little Golden children's books – feature loads of innovative variations on traditional dishes. Weekends are *wildly* popular, so try to visit on a weekday. Always get the pulled-pork 'manwich'. (08-9271 6690; www.mrsscafe.com.au; 178 Whatley Cres, Maylands; mains $11-23; 7am-4pm Mon-Fri, from 8am Sat & Sun)

El Público

MEXICAN $$

7 MAP P74, A2

Interesting and authentic spins on Mexican street food, all served as small plates that are perfect for sharing. Menu standouts include duck carnitas tacos, grilled octopus, and a sweetcorn sundae with coconut and popcorn for dessert. Bring along a few friends and groove to the occasional DJs over mezcal and great cocktails.

Mount Lawley Architecture

Into architecture, much? Mount Lawley offers up some classic examples of Australian art-deco design along Beaufort St, and beautiful Federation-era houses in the back blocks. In particular, the leafy streets east of the Beaufort St/Walcott St intersection host some gorgeous Federation villas (aka Queen Ann style), built in the 1890s and early 1900s and characterised by red brickwork, terracotta-tiled roofs, white-painted timber work and wrap-around verandas. Hot tip: book a B&B room at **Durack House** (08-9370 4305; www.durackhouse.com.au; 7 Almondbury Rd, Mount Lawley; r $195-215; P ❄) if you want to explore this lovely neighbourhood.

Back at the Beaufort St/Walcott St intersection, check out the art-deco Astor (p80) theatre (1939) and the streamlined, mod **Alexander Buildings** (1938) and **Beaucott Buildings** (also 1938...love the font!) on the same street corner. Also on Beaufort St, the Flying Scotsman (p79) pub is another art-deco beauty, built in 1934. For more on Mount Lawley's art-deco heritage and art deco right across Perth, see www.perthartdeco.net.au.

(📞0418 187 708; www.elpublico.com.au; 511 Beaufort St, Highgate; snacks & shared plates $5-19; ⏰5pm-midnight Mon-Fri, from 4pm Sat & Sun)

Mary Street Bakery

CAFE **$$**

8 MAP P74, A2

Crunchy and warm baked goods, artisanal bread and interesting cafe fare combine with what may be Perth's best chocolate-filled doughnuts at this spacious, sunny addition to the casual dining scene in Highgate. It's a good way to start the day – particularly if you order the fried-chicken buttermilk pancakes – before exploring the area's eclectic retail scene. (📞0499-509-300; www.marystreetbakery.com.au; 507 Beaufort St, Highgate; mains $13-24; ⏰7am-4pm)

Tarts

CAFE **$$**

9 MAP P74, A5

Choose from massive tarts piled with berries, apples or lime curd; rich scrambled eggs tumbling off thickly sliced sourdough; and reviving Buddha bowls. It's packed like a picnic hamper on weekends, as Northbridge locals make the most of their time out. (📞08-9328-6607; www.tartscafe.com.au; 212 Lake St, Highgate; mains $11-25; ⏰7am-3.30pm Mon-Fri, to 4.30pm Sat & Sun)

Chu Bakery

CAFE, BAKERY **$**

10 MAP P74, B4

Chu makes a great stop before or after exploring nearby Hyde Park. The coffee is excellent, the doughnuts superb, and the sourdough bread recommended if you're planning a beach picnic at Cottesloe or City Beach. For a picnic lunch, a favourite outdoor combo is takeaway espresso and toast topped with creamy avocado, whipped feta and sriracha sauce. (📞08-9328 4740; www.instagram.com/chubakery; 498 William St, Highgate; snacks from $5; ⏰7am-4pm Tue-Sun)

Local Eats

For Perthites who don't live in Highgate or Mount Lawley, the main reason to come here is to eat. And for you the visitor, the local bakeries, cafes, Mediterranean kitchens, Mexican cantinas, vegan diners and stylish Mod Oz food rooms will remove any ongoing issues you may have with your hunger. This is a place where breakfast readily morphs into lunch; where a few hours in the park flows naturally into predinner drinks, then dinner. Eating here is a pleasure.

Veggie Mama

VEGETARIAN **$**

11 MAP P74, B1

Loads of vegan and gluten-free options shine at this cute corner cafe where flavour is definitely not compromised. The menu includes delicious salads, smoothies, veggie curries and burgers; weekend breakfasts are very popular. (08-9227 1910; www.facebook.com/veggiemama01; cnr Beaufort & Vincent Sts, Mount Lawley; mains $10-20; 8am-6pm Mon, to 8pm Tue, to 9pm Wed-Sat, to 7pm Sun;)

Source Foods

CAFE $$

12 MAP P74, B6

An unassuming corner cafe committed to sustainable practices, Source Food has excellent breakfast options that include a massive spring-onion and feta-chilli scramble. The miso-mushroom with smoked eggplant hummus is a top choice for lunch. It's away from the main bustle of Northbridge, so expect a longer walk here. (08-6468 7100; www.sourcefoods.com.au; 289 Beaufort St, Highgate; mains $14-22; 7am-3pm Mon-Sat, from 7.30am Sun;)

Drinking

Swallow

WINE BAR

13 MAP P74, D3

Channelling an art-deco ambience with funky lampshades and vintage French advertising, tiny Swallow is the kind of place you'd love as your local. Wine and cocktails are exemplary, and the drinks list includes Spanish lagers, New Zealand dark beers and WA ciders. Check the website for live music Thursday to Sunday. Excellent bar snacks ($4 to $34) are also available. (08-9272 4428; www.swallowbar.com.au; 198 Whatley Cres, Maylands; 5-10pm Wed, to

Mary Street Bakery (p77)

Park Life

Highgate and Mount Lawley have some lovely leafy backstreets, but if you're not a local you mightn't have cause to venture into these shady enclaves. Instead, head for the park: gently undulating Hyde Park (p75) is great for the kids (ponds, playground, water park), while the open lawns of **Birdwood Park** (Beaufort St, Highgate) and the manicured grass tennis courts and huge Moreton Bay fig trees in **Robertson Park** (Palmerston St, Highgate) are a sight to behold. **Forrest Park** (Harold St, Mount Lawley) is where the local school kids get their soccer game on; there's a running track around the outside and some built-in gym equipment if you feel like sweating it out too. Down by the Swan River, **Banks Reserve** (off Gardiner St, Mount Lawley) is a top spot for a picnic. Follow the waterside **Tony di Scerni Pathway** along the riverbank heading upstream from here (Big Tone is credited with ensuring that Banks Reserve survived as a public open space).

11pm Thu, 4pm-midnight Fri, noon-11pm Sat, to 9pm Sun)

Five Bar CRAFT BEER

14 MAP P74, B1

International and Australian craft beers – including seasonal and one-off brews from WA's best – as well as comfy lounges and funky decor make Mount Lawley's Five Bar worth seeking out, both for the discerning drinker and the social butterfly. Wine lovers are also well catered for, and the menu leans towards classy comfort food. (08-9227 5200; www.fivebar.com.au; 560 Beaufort St, Mount Lawley; 4-10pm Mon-Thu, to midnight Fri, from noon Sat, to 10pm Sun)

Must Winebar WINE BAR

With cool French house music pulsing through the air and the perfect glass of wine in your hand (40 offerings by the glass, and more than 500 on the list), Must, which is also a restaurant (see 3 Map p74, A1) is hard to beat. It's particularly popular with mature-age bon vivants who love the bubbles and charcuterie, and upstairs is an exclusive, bookings-only Champagne bar. (08-9328 8255; www.must.com.au; 519 Beaufort St, Highgate; noon-midnight)

Flying Scotsman PUB

15 MAP P74, D3

An old-style pub that attracts the Beaufort St indie crowd, the Flying Scotsman is a good spot for a drink before a comedy show or music gig up the road at the Astor (p80) theatre. (08-9328 6200; www.facebook.com/theflyingscotto; 639 Beaufort St, Mount Lawley;

11am-midnight Sun-Tue, to 12.30am Wed-Thu, to 1am Fri, to 2am Sat)

Clarences

COCKTAIL BAR

16 MAP P74, B1

Clarences' combination of small-bar buzz, inventive cocktails and intimate bistro dining makes it a dependable spot for good times along Mount Lawley's Beaufort St strip. The menu is fiercely seasonal with a focus on flame-licked meats and vegetables. For $20 you'll get a mixed-grill extravaganza on Wednesdays and Thursdays. (08-9228 9474; www.clarences.com.au; 566 Beaufort St, Mount Lawley; 5pm-midnight Wed & Thu, from 4pm Fri, from 1pm Sat & Sun)

Velvet Lounge

BAR

Out the back of the Flying Scotsman (see 15 Map p74, D3) is this small, red-velvet-clad lounge with ska, punk and indie beats. Infinite Jest comedy nights take place on the last Monday of each month at 7pm ($10). (08-9328 6200; www.facebook.com/thevelvetloungeperth; 639 Beaufort St, Mount Lawley; noon-midnight)

Entertainment

Astor

CONCERT VENUE

17 MAP P74, D3

The beautiful art-deco Astor no longer screens films but is used for concerts and comedy gigs. (08-9370 1777; www.astortheatreperth.com; 659 Beaufort St, Mount Lawley)

Maggie Rogers performing at the Astor

MATT JELONEK/CONTRIBUTOR/GETTY IMAGES ©

Maylands Rising

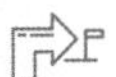

So you've cruised through Highgate's parks and enjoyed Mount Lawley's bars...what's next? Curving into the Swan River immediately east of Mount Lawley is Maylands – an uvula-shaped peninsula with a quirky industrial heritage (a brickworks and an airport). It's fast becoming the go-to 'burb for cool kids who've been priced out of Leederville, Subiaco, Mount Lawley and Fremantle. Take a few hours to snoop around: there are some great cafes around Maylands train station and along Eighth Ave, some lush parks and walking trails down on the river flats, and even a public golf course (www.maylandsgolf.com.au).

Lazy Susan's Comedy Den

COMEDY

18 MAP P74, C6

Shapiro Tuesday offers a mix of first-timers, seasoned amateurs and pros trying out new shtick (for a very reasonable $5). Friday is for more grown-up stand-ups, including some interstate visitors ($25). Saturday is the Big Hoohaa – a team-based, improv-comedy-meets-theatre laugh-fest ($25). (08-9328 2543; www.lazysusans.com.au; Brisbane Hotel, 292 Beaufort St, Highgate; 8pm Tue, Fri & Sat)

Shopping

Planet Books

BOOKS, MUSIC

19 MAP P74, D3

Cool bookshop with prints, posters and a good range of Australian-themed titles. (08-9328 7464; www.planetbooks.com.au; 638 Beaufort St, Mount Lawley; 10am-late)

CASH
only

Leederville

Little Leederville is a much-loved inner-city enclave with a kickin' cafe scene and lots of city hippies, bearded dudes and bohemian types wandering about. It hasn't always been so lovable: the local cinema once specialised in movies of a carnal bent, and the pub was known as the 'Seedy Leedy'. But these days Leederville delivers fabulous eats, drinks and quirky shops.

The Short List

- ***Oxford St cafes (p87)*** *Filling a morning (and then an afternoon) mooching between cafes and restaurants.*
- ***Leederville Hotel (p90)*** *Spending a night drinking, eating and carousing at Leederville's endearing old red-brick pub.*
- ***Lake Monger (p87)*** *Kicking a ball around, reading a book under a tree or circumnavigating the lake.*
- ***Luna (p90)*** *Catching a classic or art-house flick at this lovely art-deco cinema.*
- ***Live music (p90)*** *Tuning in to Leederville's sonics at live-music rooms.*

Getting There & Away

Leederville Station (Joondalup line) is at the bottom of Oxford St.

Bus 15 travels from the Perth Busport up Newcastle St then Oxford St. The free green CAT bus runs to Leederville train station.

Jump in a cab from Central Perth – a 10-minute ride.

Neighbourhood Map on p86

Green's & Co (p87) FLEUR BAINGER/LONELY PLANET ©

Walking Tour

Leederville Like a Local

Leederville is what every big city needs: a neighbourhood enclave of cafes, restaurants, bars and shops with a distinctly boho, offbeat vibe. Perth's urban culture does lean too far towards the mainstream at times, but Leederville offers sweet relief for anyone arty, subversive or just a bit different. Hang out at local haunts and catch the Leederville vibe.

Walk Facts

Start cnr Melrose & Oxford Sts; bus route 15

End Lake Monger; bus route 15

Length 2km; one hour

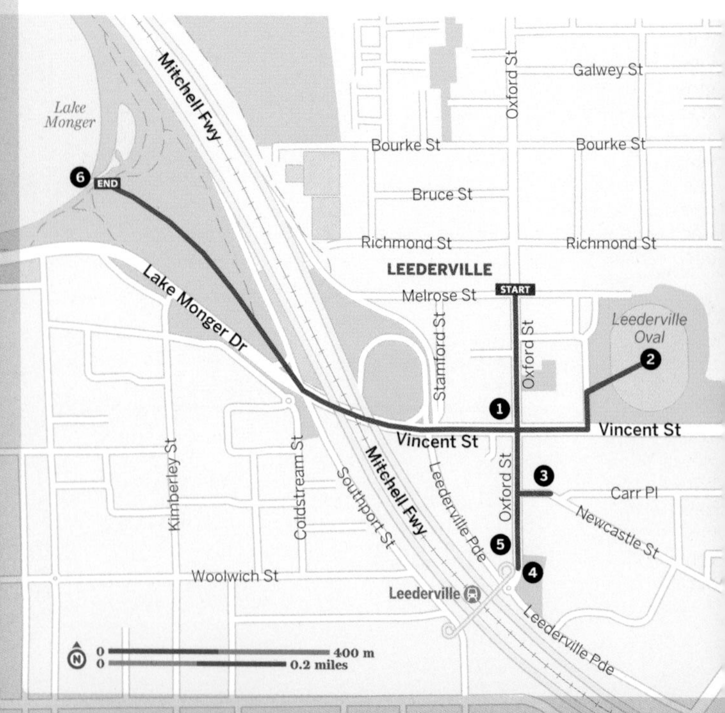

❶ Luna Cinema

From Melrose St, head down Oxford St to the Luna (p90) cinema on the Vincent St corner. Like all Australian cities, Perth has lost most of its charming old neighbourhood cinemas to a tide of multiscreen megaplexes...but not the Luna! This art-deco art-house cinema has been here since 1927, when movies were still silent. Check out the awesome Vincent St mural.

❷ Leederville Oval

Oxford St's effervescence is tempting, but for now, turn left onto Vincent St towards the **Leederville Oval**. This lush ground hosts the East Perth Royals football team, who compete in the West Australian Football League (WAFL; www.wafl.com.au). The Royals haven't been playing particularly regally of late, but have won the comp 17 times and inspire deep passions in Leederville locals.

❸ Leederville Hotel

Cross Vincent St, backtrack to Oxford St, turn left and cruise the cafes. If you've been thinking, 'You know, all these cafes are great, but where's the pub?', turn left onto Newcastle St. The lovely old red-brick Leederville Hotel (p90) has been beering it up since 1897, and has recently morphed into several venues under one roof. Hit the bar at Bill's.

❹ Oxford St Reserve

Return to Oxford St and cool your boots at the bottom end of the main drag, where lovely little **Oxford St Reserve** awaits. Local mums and dads and their artfully dressed kids rampage around the shady nature-play area here, then retreat to the adjunct cafe to discuss composting techniques and fair-trade coffee.

❺ Kailis Bros

'I'm on a seafood diet: I see food, then I eat it.' Jokes aside, for some of WA's best seafood, head back up the western side of Oxford St and into Kailis Bros (p88). Established in 1926 (on Oxford St since 2000), Kailis is the place for some fresh red emperor, flame snapper or blue swimmer crabs to take away.

❻ Lake Monger

Further up Oxford St, turn left on Vincent St and cross below the Mitchell Fwy. Ahead is the rather unappealingly named Lake Monger (p87) and its surrounding parkland – Leederville's green heartland. There's a 3.8km track around the lake if you feel like walking further, but hey, this is Leederville – wouldn't you rather read a book under a tree?

For reviews see

Sights	p87
Eating	p87
Drinking	p90
Entertainment	p90
Shopping	p91

0 400 m
0 0.2 miles

A B C D E F
1 2 3 4

LEEDERVILLE
NORTH PERTH
Charles Veryard Reserve
Beatty Park
Beatty Park Leisure Centre
Beatty Lodge
Leederville Oval
Keith Frame Park
Dorrien Gardens
Leederville

Loftus St
Charles St
Vincent St
Fitzgerald St
Bulwer St
Throssell St
Cowle St
Carr St
Kingston Ave
Newcastle St
Carr Pl
Oxford St
Leederville Pde
Mitchell Fwy
Stamford St
Melrose St
Richmond St
Bruce St
Scott St
Bourke St
Galwey St
Tennyson St
Kadina St
Barnett St
Kayle St
Farr Ave
Florence St
Alfonso St
Claverton St
Leake St
Raglan Rd
Alma Rd
View St
Vine St
Albert St
Angove St

Sights

Lake Monger

PARK

1 MAP P86, A3

In spring black swans and their cygnets waddle about the grounds – a meeting place for local birdlife – nonplussed by joggers circling the lake on the flat, 3.5km path surrounded by grass. The lake is walking distance from Leederville train station; exit on the side opposite the shops, turn right onto Southport St and veer left onto Lake Monger Dr. (Lake Monger Dr)

Beatty Park Leisure Centre

SWIMMING

2 MAP P86, D3

Built for the Commonwealth Games, hosted by Perth in 1962, this complex has indoor and outdoor pools, water slides and a huge gym. Turn left at the top of William St and continue on Vincent St to just past Charles St. (08-9273 6080; www.beattypark.com.au; 220 Vincent St, North Perth; swimming adult/child $7/5; 5.30am-9pm Mon-Fri, 6.30am-7pm Sat & Sun;)

Eating

Pinchos

TAPAS $

3 MAP P86, A4

Iberian-inspired good times constantly rock this corner location amid Leederville's many cafes, casual restaurants and bars. The must-have tapas are the pork-belly chicharrones and the Piedro Ximenez and blue-cheese mushrooms – they've never left the menu. Those and the beef cheeks are perfect drinking fodder with the attractively priced Spanish beer, wine, sherry and on-tap sangria.

The feed-me menu, from $39, is one of the best value in Perth. (08-9228 3008; www.pinchos.me; 112-124 Oxford St; small plates $11-18, larger plates $25-27; 8am-10pm Sun-Tue, to 10.30pm Wed-Thu, to 11pm Fri & Sat)

Green's & Co

CAFE $

4 MAP P86, A4

The coffee may be mediocre but the vibe is chill, care of hundreds of spherical, white paper lampshades swaying in the breeze. Plonk down on one of the many Ikea couches and find your favourite band on the posters coating the walls, as you dive into a 'how-do-I-choose?' selection of cakes. Kids love the coin slot rides out the back. (08-9444 4093; www.facebook.com/greensleederville; 123 Oxford St; cakes $5-10; 6.30am-11pm Mon-Thu, to midnight Fri, from 7am Sat, 8am-11pm Sun;)

Duende

TAPAS $$

5 MAP P86, B4

Sleek, candlelit Duende occupies a quiet corner site just off the buzzing nexus of Leederville. Stellar, modern-accented and good-value tapas offer a compelling argument

Perth's Commonwealth Games

Many Australians outside of WA might struggle to recall very much about the 1962 British Empire and Commonwealth Games (the 'Commonwealth Games' for short), held in Perth. And indeed, the main arena, Perry Lakes Stadium in Floreat, is no more, replaced by the Western Australian Athletics Stadium in 2009. The Lake Monger Velodrome in Leederville is now a soccer stadium. But a stone's (or perhaps javelin's) throw from Leederville, the Beatty Park Leisure Centre (p87) is still around: this was the venue for the Games' swimming events, with swimmers housed across the street at what is now **Beatty Lodge** (Map p86, D3; 08-9227 1521; www.beattylodge.com.au; 235 Vincent St, West Perth).

Predictably, Australia dominated the games' medal tally with 105 shiny metal discs of various metallurgic compositions, scooping the Beatty Park pool (pun intended) with 15 golds. Even if most of the venues are long gone, world-beating swims by the likes of Dawn Fraser, Murray Rose and Iain O'Brien live on in Leederville's collective sporting memory.

to make a meal of it. Or call in for a late-night glass of dessert wine and churros. The cocktails are particularly polished here too. The six-course chef's selection menu makes so much sense ($55). (08-9228 0123; www.duende.com.au; 662 Newcastle St; tapas & mains $8-20; noon-late Mon-Fri, from 11.30am Sat & Sun)

Kailis Bros SEAFOOD $$

6 MAP P86, A4

A big fresh-seafood supplier with attached cafe. Go in just for a stickybeak: the staff are always happy to pick up a live yabby or marron (local freshwater crayfish) to show interested parties. The fish market also has a poke-bowl window, with sashimi-grade fish sliced from specimens brought in that morning. (08-9443 6300; www.kailisbrosleederville.com.au; 101 Oxford St; small plates $14-26, mains $28-60; poke bowls $16; shop 8am-6pm, cafe 7am-late, poke window 10am-2pm Mon-Sat)

Sayers CAFE $$

7 MAP P86, B4

This classy Leederville brunch cafe has a counter groaning under the weight of an alluring cake selection. The excellent breakfast menu includes coffee spiced brisket with fried eggs and sesame-seed bagel, while lunch highlights include house-smoked salmon in saffron rice with poached eggs. Welcome to one of Perth's best cafes. (08-

9227 0429; www.sayersfood.com.au; 224 Carr Pl; mains $17-27; 7am-5pm)

Kitsch

ASIAN $$

8 MAP P86, A2

Southeast Asian–style street food, Thai beers and a light-strung frangipani tree make Kitsch a great spot for a few laid-back hours of tasty grazing. Expect to stay (and eat) longer than planned. It has good specials too: on Tuesdays score a pad thai and beer for $20; on Wednesdays it's a wok creation and cocktail for $21. (08-9242 1229; www.kitschbar.com.au; 229 Oxford St; shared plates $11-29; 5pm-late Tue-Sat)

Low Key Chow House

ASIAN $$

9 MAP P86, A3

Noisy and bustling – just like the Southeast Asian street-food places it references – eating at Low Key Chow House is a fun experience best shared with a group. Sip cold Singha beer or punchy Asian cocktails, and order up a storm from a menu featuring the best of Malaysia, Vietnam, Thailand, Cambodia and Laos. Tip: get the dumplings. (08-9443 9305; www.keepitlowkey.com.au; 140 Oxford St; share plates $5-24, mains $26-34; 5.30-10pm Tue-Thu, noon-3pm & 5.30-10.30pm Sat & Sun)

Jus Burgers

BURGERS $

10 MAP P86, A4

Tasty gourmet burgers and sliders made from 100% local, never frozen produce. There's another branch in **Subiaco** (08-9381 1895; 1 Rokeby Rd; burgers $6-17; 11am-late). (08-9228 2230; www.jusburgers.com.au; 743 Newcastle St; burgers $12-16; 11am-late)

Market Juicery

CAFE $

11 MAP P86, A3

Superfood smoothies, cold-pressed juices and zingy salads all feature at this good-value lunch stop amid the funky retailers of Leederville. Wraps and bagels are also appealing. You'll the find the Juicery down an arcade behind the magazine shop. (0458 877 000; www.facebook.com/themarketjuicery; shop 2, 139-141 Oxford St; salads $10-12, juices & smoothies $8-9; 7am-3pm Mon-Fri, 8am-2pm Sat;)

Trams & Trolleybuses

Like many Australian cities, Perth had an extensive tram network through the first half of the 20th century, operating from 1899 to 1958. Trams were gradually replaced by trolleybuses (electric buses), which were in turn phased out by 1969 in favour of regulation petrol-powered buses. Walking along Newcastle St and Oxford St today, it's not hard to imagine the Leederville tram rumbling through – it would have been an atmospheric.

Drinking

Leederville Hotel

PUB

12 MAP P86, A4

Cool decor and good food ensure nights are huge at the Garden, the Leederville's stab at a 21st-century gastropub. It's the summery, open-air section to the enormous pub: the rest is filled by **Bill's Bar**, a polished-concrete and couches zone, while out the back is the popular **Blue Flamingo**, which heaves after dark. Live music plays upstairs at **Babushka**. (08-9202 8282; www.leedervillehotel.com; 742 Newcastle St; 11am-late)

Entertainment

Luna

CINEMA

13 MAP P86, A3

This fully licensed, art-house cinema has Monday doubleheader features and a bar. The vintage cinema has been renovated with four new screens alongside the original building. Cheap tickets on Wednesday ($12 to $14). During summer there's an outdoor screen. (08-9444 4056; www.lunapalace.com.au; 155 Oxford St)

Rosemount Hotel

LIVE MUSIC

14 MAP P86, F1

Local and international bands play regularly in this spacious

Luna

Long Live the Luna

One of Perth's last remaining suburban picture houses, the Luna in Leederville has a long and convoluted history. Opened in 1927 as the New Oxford Theatre to a full house of 1286 delighted locals, this art-deco delight moved through the era of silent movies to become Perth's first cinema with sound. After a string of different owners and name changes – the Nickelodeon, the Olympia, the Star Theatre – and periods where the cinema only screened Italian and Greek and then R-rated movies, the Luna name arrived in the 1990s as local tastes shifted towards the indie and art-house films screening here today. Don't miss it!

art-deco pub with a laid-back beer garden. (08-9328 7062; www.rosemounthotel.com.au; cnr Angove & Fitzgerald Sts; 11am-late)

Shopping

Future Shelter — HOMEWARES

15 MAP P86, F1

Quirky clothing, gifts and homewares designed and manufactured locally. Surrounding Angove St is an emerging hip North Perth neighbourhood with other cafes and design shops worth browsing. (08-9228 4832; www.futureshelter.com; 56 Angove St, North Perth; 10am-5pm Mon-Sat, noon-3pm Sun)

Atlas Divine — CLOTHING

16 MAP P86, A4

Cool women's and men's clobber: jeans, quirky tees, dresses etc. (08-9242 5880; www.facebook.com/atlasdivine; 121 Oxford St; 10am-5pm Sat-Wed, to 9pm Thu & Fri)

CLOUGH

Kings Park & Subiaco

To have an expanse of parks and bushland as vast as Kings Park so close to a major Australian city is truly remarkable. This place is big – bigger than New York City's Central Park, actually! Once you find your way out, head into Subiaco for multicultural eats and a clutch of good galleries and theatres in which to recivilise yourself.

The Short List

- ***Kings Park (p94)*** *Exploring this wonderland of wildflowers, parks and bushland.*
- ***Rokeby Rd restaurants (p100)*** *Deciding where to go for coffee, for lunch, for dinner...*
- ***Subiaco Farmers Market (p100)*** *Easing into the weekend at this chilled-out Saturday-morning market.*
- ***Aboriginal art (p103)*** *Browsing Subiaco's commercial galleries.*
- ***Outdoor cinema (p102)*** *Rolling out a picnic rug at an outdoor movie in the park.*

Getting There & Around

Bus 28 runs to Subiaco from Perth Busport; bus 935 runs to the Kings Park entrance on Fraser Ave from St Georges Tce.

On the Fremantle line, Subiaco Station caps the end of Rokeby Rd.

Kings Park is a 1km uphill walk from St Georges Tce in the city. Walking to Subiaco from the city is also possible (around 3.5km).

Neighbourhood Map on p98

Kings Park (p94) MANFRED GOTTSCHALK/GETTY IMAGES ©

Top Sight

Kings Park

Just to the west of Central Perth, Kings Park is the main sight to see around this neck of the woods… but what a sight it is! Technically called Kings Park & Botanic Garden, it's a 400-hectare spread of neat parklands and marvellously scruffy native bush, resting atop Mt Eliza (more of a hill, really). Give yourself a day to explore.

MAP P98, D4

08-9480 3600

www.bgpa.wa.gov.au

admission free

free guided walks 10am, noon & 2pm

Kaarta Gar-up

The Wadjuk people knew this area as Kaarta Gar-up and used it for thousands of years for hunting, food gathering, ceremonies, teaching and tool-making. A freshwater spring at the base of the escarpment, now known as Kennedy Fountain but before that as Goonininup, was a home of the Wargal, mystical snakelike creatures that created the Swan River and other waterways.

Park Life

Today the 400-hectare, bush-filled expanse of Kings Park, smack in the city centre and enjoying epic views, is Perth's pride and joy. The Botanic Garden contains over 3000 plant species indigenous to WA, including a **giant boab tree**. The boab is dearly loved by the people of WA: it travelled 3200km on the back of a truck to arrive in its new home, and is a 750-year-old symbol of the Kimberley.

Each September the free Kings Park Festival (p102) displays the state's famed wildflowers. A year-round highlight is the **Lotterywest Federation Walkway** (pictured left), a 620m path leading to a 222m-long glass-and-steel sky bridge that crosses a canopy of eucalyptus trees.

The main road leading into the park, Fraser Ave, is lined with towering lemon-scented gums that are dramatically lit at night. At its culmination are the **State War Memorial**, a cafe, a gift shop, **Fraser's restaurant** and the **Kings Park Visitor Centre**. Free guided walks leave from here.

The park is a great spot for a picnic or to let the kids off the leash in one of the playgrounds. Its numerous tracks are popular with walkers and joggers all year round, with an ascent of the steep Jacob's Ladder (p101) stairs from the river rewarded with wonderful views.

★ Top Tips

- Visit Fraser Ave at dawn to watch mist rise from the Swan River.
- Come into the Botanic Garden after dark to marvel at the city centre's urban glow.
- There is a handful of excellent playground zones that local families love. Hit up the May Drive Parkland, the Saw Avenue Picnic Area, the Ivey Watson Playground and the Rio Tinto Naturescape.
- There is a variety of free walks that depart daily, at 10am, noon and 2pm.

Take a Break

Have a basic cafe meal with views at Botanical Cafe or go a bit more upmarket with Fraser's (p100) restaurant (which is best enjoyed with the evening vista).

Walking Tour

Subiaco Streetwise

Subiaco – a name bestowed by Benedictine monks, homesick for the Italian town near Rome – is an affluent and at times rather staid enclave. But scratch the surface and you'll find some interesting history here too (sporting, architectural and otherwise), plus some offbeat local foodie undercurrents surfacing at the weekly farmers market. Take a walk and explore.

Walk Facts

Start Subiaco Oval; Subiaco Station

End Kings Park; bus route 935

Length 3km; 90 minutes

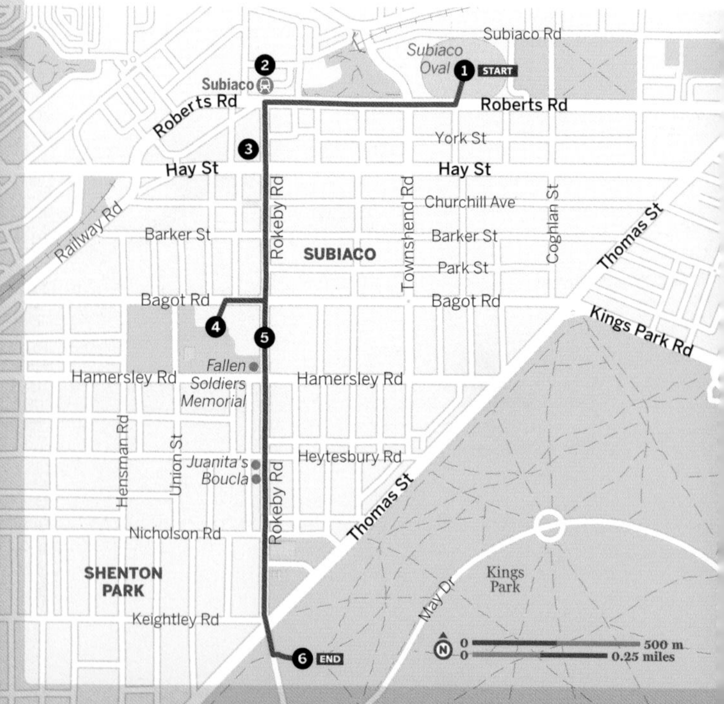

❶ Subiaco Oval

Until recently, historic Subiaco Oval (aka Domain Stadium) was the home ground of both the West Coast Eagles and Fremantle Dockers AFL football teams. Then Optus Stadium (p46) opened in Burswood in 2018, and old 'Subi' was surplus to requirements – a huge cultural and economic loss for Subiaco. Property developers are circling: are the wrecking balls swinging yet?

❷ Subiaco Square

Cheer up: further west along Roberts Rd, contemporary Subiaco is alive and kicking at Subiaco Square, an up-to-the-minute shopping and residential complex above Subiaco Station. Sushi bars, burger joints and a huge supermarket compete for your custom – not as soulful as the adjacent Subiaco Station Street Markets that closed in 2015, but like Subiaco itself, the vibe is perfectly civil.

❸ Regal Theatre

Wow, what a beauty! A few blocks south along Rokeby Rd (pronounced rock-uh-bee) on the corner of Hay St, Regal Theatre (p102) is a handsome art-deco theatre. Built in 1938 as a cinema, it was converted to a live-performance theatre in 1977. With room for 1000 bums on seats, it hosts comedy, musicals and cheesy rock tribute shows.

❹ Subiaco Farmers Market

Eyeball the estimable old Subiaco Hotel (1897) across the intersection then truck south along Rokeby Rd past shops, cafes and plenty of plane trees. Every Saturday morning, locals make a beeline for Subiaco Primary School on Bagot Rd where the left-field Subiaco Farmers Market (p100) sets up shop. Breakfast bites, dubious buskers and organic fruit and veg – it's all here.

❺ Rokeby Rd

Back on Rokeby Rd, check out the noble Fallen Soldiers Memorial clocktower (1923) on the corner of Hamersley Rd. The pick of Subiaco's eating and drinking dens extend south from here, mostly beyond the Heytesbury Rd intersection. Swing into amicable Juanita's (p101) for a quick drink with the regulars, or Boucla (p100) cafe for some Greek-inspired tarts and salads.

❻ Kings Park

A true Perth highlight resides in verdant splendour on the end of Rokeby Rd: Kings Park (p94) is where Subiaco locals come to jog, meditate, picnic, kick a ball and walk the dog. The road into the park is a palm-lined avenue with rolling lawns on either side: pick a spot and do as the locals do.

A B C D E F
1 2 3 4

Mitchell Fwy
Sutherland St
1 Scitech
City West
Roe St
Railway St
Delhi St
Wellington St
Murray St
Thomas St
WEST PERTH
Outram St
Hay St
Richardson St
Colin St
Havelock St
Parliament Pl
Ord St
Ventnor Ave
Walker Ave
Kings Park Rd
Malcolm St
Cliff St
Quest Mounts Bay Road
Mounts Bay Rd
Jacobs Ladder
Fraser Ave
13
6
12
Mt Eliza Reservoir
May Dr
Kings Park
Subiaco Rd
West Leederville
Railway Pde
Subiaco Oval
Roberts Rd
York St
Hay St
14
Coghlan St
Churchill Ave
Barker St
Park St
Bagot Rd
Townshend Rd
SUBIACO
Hamersley Rd
Thomas St
Catherine St
Salisbury St
Subiaco
Station St
Hood St
Railway Rd
10
Rokeby Rd
4
7
2
3
Heytesbury Rd
Bagot Rd
5
9
Barker St
Union St
Hensman Rd
Centro Ave
Hay St
Railway Rd
Hamersley Rd
Nicholson Rd
SHENTON PARK
Keightley Rd

For reviews see
Top Sights p94
Sights p100
Eating p100
Drinking p101
Entertainment p102
Shopping p102
0 500 m
0 0.25 miles
A
B
C
D
E
F
5
6
7
8
Kings Park
Botanic Garden
Broadwalk Vista
Lovekin Dr
Forrest Dr
May Dr
Poole Ave
Park Ave
Lotterywest Federation Walkway
Mounts Bay Rd
Riverside Dr
Narrows Bridge
Kwinana Fwy
Mill Point Rd
Judd St
SOUTH PERTH
Swan River
Matilda Bay
CRAWLEY
Stirling Hwy
Winthrop Ave
Thomas St
Onslow Rd
11
8

Sights

Scitech

MUSEUM

1 MAP P98, F1

Scitech is an excellent rainy-day option for those travelling with children. It has over 160 hands-on, large-scale science and technology exhibits. Tickets are discounted later in the afternoon. (08-9215 0700; www.scitech.org.au; City West Centre, Sutherland St, West Perth; adult/child $19/12; 9am-4pm Mon-Fri, 9.30am-5pm Sat & Sun;)

Eating

Boucla

CAFE $

2 MAP P98, B4

A locals' secret, this Greek- and Levantine-infused haven is pleasingly isolated from the thick of the Rokeby Rd action. Baklava and cakes tempt you from the corner, and huge tarts filled with blue-vein cheese and roast vegetables spill off plates. The salads are great too. (08-9381 2841; www.boucla.com.au; 349 Rokeby Rd, Subiaco; mains $10-23; 7am-4pm Mon-Sat, 8am-1pm Sun)

Meeka

MIDDLE EASTERN $$$

3 MAP P98, B4

In Subiaco's Rokeby Rd restaurant enclave, Meeka combines Modern Australian cuisine with the flavours of the Middle East and North Africa. Of the many meze dishes try the local tempura whiting with eggplant puree and pomegranate salad, while a lamb tagine will send you home full-bellied. At $60, the chef's multi-course menu is excellent value. (08-9381 1800; www.meekarestaurant.com.au; 361 Rokeby Rd, Subiaco; meze $15-18, mains $31-39; 5pm-late Tue-Sat)

Chez Jean-Claude Patisserie

BAKERY $

4  MAP P98, B3

Line up with locals for brioche, sandwich baguettes and other baked goodies at this Subiaco bakery – it always smells amazing as you walk by. (08-9381 7968; www.chezjeanclaudepatisserie.com.au; 333 Rokeby Rd, Subiaco; snacks $3-10; 6am-6pm Mon-Fri, 7.30am-1.30pm Sat)

Subiaco Farmers Market

MARKET $

Every Saturday morning this market fills with gourmet-food stalls, fresh fruit and veg, naturally leavened breads, fresh flowers, pretty cupcakes and live music from buskers. Bring along your dog if you want to really blend in with the locals. (0406 758 803; www.subifarmersmarket.com.au; Subiaco Primary School, 271 Bagot Rd; snacks & meals $7-12; 8am-noon Sat;)

Fraser's

MODERN AMERICAN $$$

6 MAP P98, E4

Atop Kings Park, overlooking the city and the glittering Swan River,

Climbing Jacob's Ladder

The view of Central Perth from atop Kings Park (p94; technically a summit called Mt Eliza) is an absolute show-stopper. The temptation is to launch yourself down from the park and into the city...but wait – there's an enormous cliff-face in the way! This very problem was solved in 1909 when the industrious Joseph Huck & Sons won the contract to build a staircase down the precipice, following the detailed designs of the Perth City Engineer, Mr Henry Payne. The Hucks cobbled together 274 jarrah steps down the steep 46m incline, landing at sea level behind the present-day **Quest Mounts Bay Road** (Map p98, F4; 08-9480 8100; www.questapartments.com.au; 130 Mounts Bay Rd) apartments.

Christened **Jacob's Ladder** after the biblical flight of steps from Earth up to heaven, the new staircase was hugely popular, before splinters, rusty nails and wood rot forced its closure in 1961. It took a few years to rebuild, but the revised 242-step concrete stair has (despite a brief closure in 2016) stood the test of time – to the considerable irritation of local residents, who awaken at dawn to the sounds of asthmatic joggers outside their bedroom windows.

Fraser's is in a wonderful location. Thankfully, the food is also reasonably good, making it a popular spot for business lunches and romantic dinners on the terrace on balmy summer nights. (08-9481 7100; www.frasersrestaurant.com.au; Fraser Ave, Kings Park; mains $32-45; noon-late Mon-Fri, from 11.30am Sat & Sun)

Drinking

Juanita's

BAR

7 MAP P98, B3

Welcome to Perth's most neighbourly small bar. Tapas, shared platters (terrines, pâtés and fries – the co-owner chef often works the floor) and a concise selection of beer and wine partner with mismatched chairs and couches inside, and packed clusters of tables outside. It's all thoroughly local, very charming and a refreshing antidote to the flash, renovated pubs elsewhere in Subiaco. (08-9388 8882; www.facebook.com/juanitasbarsubiaco; 341 Rokeby Rd, Subiaco; 2-10pm Tue, to 11pm Thu, from noon Fri, from 2pm Sat, 3-9pm Sun)

Entertainment

Somerville Auditorium
CINEMA

8 MAP P98, A8

A quintessential Perth experience, the Perth Festival's international film program is held outdoors on the University of WA's beautiful grounds, surrounded by pines and strings of lights. Picnicking before the film is a must. Bring a cushion as the deckchair seating can be uncomfortable. (08-6488 2000; www.perthfestival.com.au; 35 Stirling Hwy, Crawley; Nov-Mar)

Park Party

Celebrating all things floral, botanical and earthbound, the long-running **Kings Park Festival** (www.kingsparkfestival.com.au; Sep) – into its 56th year in 2019 – is the perfect excuse to explore Perth's beloved park (p94). When the native wildflowers here burst into lurid colour every September, the park is overrun with photographers, flower fans and bush boffins, walking and talking up a flowery storm. Even if you're not into wildflowers, there's yoga, coffee carts, art exhibitions, meditation sessions, tai chi, kids' activities and loads of live music – it's a great day out.

Subiaco Arts Centre
THEATRE

9 MAP P98, A3

Indoor and outdoor theatres used for drama, concerts and festival shows. (08-6212 9292; www.ptt.wa.gov.au/venues/subiaco-arts-centre; 180 Hamersley Rd, Subiaco)

Regal Theatre
THEATRE

10  MAP P98, B2

A heritage art-deco theatre hosting popular musicals, stage shows and festival events. (08-9388 2066; www.regaltheatre.com.au; 474 Hay St, Subiaco)

Moonlight Cinema
CINEMA

11  MAP P98, B6

In summer, bring a blanket and a picnic and enjoy a romantic moonlit movie. Booking ahead online is recommended. (www.moonlight.com.au; May Dr Parklands, Kings Park; 1 Dec-31 Mar)

Shopping

Aspects of Kings Park
ART, SOUVENIRS

12 MAP P98, E4

Australian art, homewares, chunky jewellery and coffee-table books with an emphasis on handcrafted pieces and organic shapes. (08-9480 3900; www.aspectsofkingspark.com.au; Fraser Ave, Kings Park; 9am-5pm)

Wildflowers, Kings Park (p94)

Aboriginal Art & Craft Gallery

ART

13 MAP P98, E4

Work from around WA; more populist than high end or collectable. The gallery is slightly hidden below the Kaarta Gar-up lookout. (08-9481 7082; www.aboriginalgallery.com.au; Fraser Ave, Kings Park; 10.30am-4.30pm Mon-Fri, 11am-4pm Sat & Sun)

Mossenson Galleries – Indigenart

ART

14 MAP P98, C2

Serious Aboriginal art from around Australia but with a focus on WA artists. Works include weavings, paintings on canvas, bark and paper, and sculpture. (08-9388 2899; www.mossensongalleries.com.au; 115 Hay St, Subiaco; 11am-4pm Wed-Sat)

Scarborough to Cottesloe

In Australia, perhaps only Sydney can rival Perth for great urban beaches. The Indian Ocean grinds in from the west, with reliable surf breaking on the glorious golden-sand coastline between Cottesloe to the south and Scarborough to the north. Cottesloe is classy and family-aligned, while 'Scarbs' is raffish and youthful. Cafes, pubs and beachy sleeps abound.

The Short List

- ***Cottesloe Beach (p106)*** *Swanning around on the sand at Perth's best beach.*
- ***Aquarium of Western Australia (p114)*** *Meeting critters from the deep at this excellent aquarium.*
- ***Scarborough Beach Pool (p116)*** *Diving into this cool pool on the Scarborough foreshore.*
- ***Cottesloe Beach Hotel (p111)*** *Kicking back with a glass of something at this fab art-deco pub.*
- ***City Beach (p114)*** *Enjoying a seaside cafe lunch at this exclusive beach.*

Getting There & Away

Scarborough is 35 minutes from Perth Busport (route 990). Cottesloe is 45 minutes from Elizabeth Quay Bus Station (route 102).

A cab from Central Perth to Scarborough or Cottesloe is 25 minutes either way.

Cottesloe is on the Fremantle line; from the station it's a 1.5km walk to the beach (or take bus 102). For Scarborough, take a Joondalup train to Stirling, then bus 421 to the beach.

Neighbourhood Map on p112

Cottesloe Beach (p106) EDEN NGUYEN/SHUTTERSTOCK ©

Top Sight

Cottesloe Beach

Cottesloe is Perth's glittering supernova among many other stars. Its smooth, pale sands are met by crystal clear ocean, while grassy terraces and shady trees means all kinds of beach-lovers are happy. A rocky groyne ensures seas are calm and, beside it, quite shallow. There are plenty of cafes and restaurants here to keep you sated between swims.

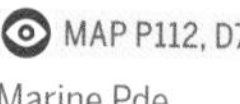
MAP P112, D7

Marine Pde

Sculpture by the Sea

Sure, the beach is magnificent for surfing, sunning and swimming...but if you're in Cottesloe in March, the annual **Sculpture by the Sea** (www.sculpturebythesea.com/cottesloe) festivities (pictured left) put a decidedly arty spin on proceedings here. All along the sea wall, across the beach and dotting the lawns towards North Cottesloe, local artists' best sculptural efforts are exhibited for public assessment. Funny, clever and provocative, it's a hugely popular event.

The Cottesloe Pylon

'Hey – what's that weird stripy spike out in the water off Cottesloe Beach?' Not an uncommon question on this stretch of the coast. Known as the Cottesloe Pylon, it's actually the last remaining piece of a shark-net support structure erected in 1925 after an elderly swimmer was killed here. The rest of the structure succumbed to storm damage and the pounding Indian Ocean surf over the years. About 100m offshore, swimming out to the Pylon is a rite of passage for Cottesloe teens, while its spike is traditionally rebranded with the colours of rival surf clubs after major tournament wins.

Cottesloe Pines

Aside from the drop-dead gorgeous beach, the defining features of Cottesloe are its towering ranks of extremely healthy-looking Norfolk Island pine trees *(Araucaria heterophylla)* lining the streets. First planted along John St in 1915 when the Cottesloe Roads Board procured 168 pint-sized pines, the 18-inch saplings did so well that the pine-planting scheme soon expanded to incorporate most of the streets behind the beach. John St and Broome St remain the prime exemplars – cast an eye skywards as you wander by.

★ Top Tips

- Arrive before 10am to see the ocean at its glassiest, before winds and the sun's reflection arrive.
- Grab fish and chips from **Amberjacks** (www.amberjacks.com.au) and picnic on the grass.
- Snorkel over the leafy reef north of the North Cottesloe Surf Lifesaving Club rooms.

Take a Break

- Il Lido (p118) Italian canteen does the area's best bistro fare – ideal for coffee or a meal, inside or out.
- The **Cottesloe Beach Club** (www.cottesloebeachhotel.com.au/spaces/the-beach-club), is a Hamptons-style oasis that's an ideal location for a few wines.
- Back from the beach, newcomer North Street Store (p118) draws crowds for drool-worthy coffee, and pork sandwiches made with house-baked bread.

Top Sight

Scarborough Beach

Scarborough is a mish-mash of surfers, backpackers, bikies, bar hoppers and families; it's quite the melting pot. It's only about 20 minutes from the city centre and despite its $100 million facelift, it retains its anything-goes nonchalance. There are casual eateries and takeaway spots aplenty along the beachfront, leading you to the new, Olympic size pool and paddling zone that's heated to 27 degrees.

MAP P112, B7

The Esplanade

The New Scarborough

When WA state premier Mark McGowan cut the ribbon on the $100 million Scarborough Beach foreshore redevelopment in 2018, the local mayor gleefully talked up Scarborough's return to prominence. In the early 2000s, the gritty 'burb had gained a rep for booze-fuelled brawling and general seediness—and the tourists were going elsewhere (Cottesloe sure is pretty). But now, with the fabulous Scarborough Beach Pool (p116), the epic Snake Pit (p117) skate bowl, a fab kids' playground (pictured left), free BBQs, new cafes and restaurants, and a network of trails and lawns, the stage is set for a more even-tempered, family-friendly Scarborough to emerge. There's also a new 40-storey 'twin towers' apartment development planned here, a few blocks back from the beach: Scarborough's economic future is looking positively effervescent! Meanwhile, oblivious to the suburb's socio-economic struggles, the Indian Ocean swell continues to roll in, same as it always has...

The Original Snake Pit

Standing on the lip of Scarborough's Snake Pit (p117) skate bowl – a 3.6m-deep concrete canyon – cast your mind back to the 1950s and '60s, when the original Snake Pit was the go-to destination for Perth's 'bodgies and widgies' (read: American 'greasers'). Like everywhere in the Western world at the time, rock and roll was blowing Perth teenagers' minds. In 1957 some teens started shamelessly dancing outside 'Ye Olde Kool-Korner Kafe' on the Scarborough foreshore. Sensing a commercial opportunity, a former US submariner called 'Big Don' corralled the kids onto an outdoor concrete terrace on the corner of Manning St and The Esplanade, cranked up a jukebox and started selling hamburgers. The Snake Pit was born...and lasted until the hippies showed up in 1969.

★ Top Tips

- Scarborough is a family playground by day, but reverts to a party haven by night; backpackers particularly enjoy its mainstream bars.
- Beware of rips in the water and swim between the flags, where the local Surf Life Saving Club patrols year-round.
- There's free wi-fi on the main beach and in the foreshore areas.

Take a Break

- Funky bar-eatery, **El Grotto** (www.elgrotto.com) serves up tacos and tequila, with live DJs regularly spinning tracks.
- Quench your thirst at the newly opened **Peach Pit** (www.thepeachpitbar.com.au), where polished cocktails are shaken in summery surrounds.

Walking Tour

Cottesloe Cruiser

Cruise the beautiful streets around Perth's best beach on this leisurely stroll from the station to the sand. There's be plenty of time and opportunity for good things to eat and drink: time your run with the sunset for a sundowner and some spectacular Indian Ocean views.

Walk Facts

Start Cottesloe Station

End Cottesloe Beach Hotel; bus route 102

Length 2.2km; two hours

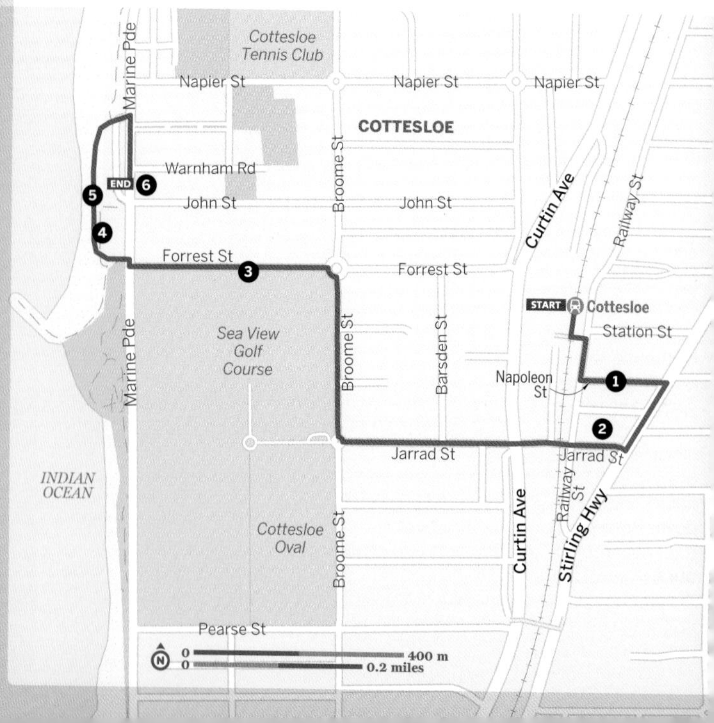

❶ Napoleon St

Cottesloe's inland commercial hub is a tight wedge of streets that's well worth a look before you head for the beach. From the Cottesloe Station platform, take the overpass heading east over the rail lines, cross Station St and turn left into **Napoleon St**, the main shopping and eating strip. Stop at a local cafe for a coffee or some other more adventurous tonic to get your feet moving.

❷ Boatshed Market

Turn right at the end of Napoleon, then right again into the car park fronting Jarrad St. Boatshed Market (p118) is here: stuff your backpack full of deli bites to eat down on the Cottesloe sand. Or, if you feel like cooking, stop here on your way home for some of Perth's best seafood.

❸ Norfolk Island Pines

Back on Jarrad St, head west over Railway St and the rail line, continuing to Broome St: the lush Cottesloe Oval and Sea View Golf Course spread out before you. Turn right and continue until you hit Forrest St: Cottesloe's famous Norfolk Island pine trees (p107) make an appearance, a verdant colonnade along Broome St and down Forrest St towards the shore (...in more scientific circles than ours, these trees are known as *Araucaria heterophylla*, if you want to impress/annoy someone at the bar). Take Forrest and truck west; some typically plush Cottesloe mansions are on your right.

❹ Indiana Cottesloe Beach

Approaching the shore, cross Marine Pde and duck down in front of the **Indiana Cottesloe Beach restaurant** (www.indiana.com.au), a magnificent piece of architectural confection that looks like it's been transplanted from some obscure 19th-century Portuguese colony (but actually dates from 1996).

❺ Cottesloe Beach

Now you're on Cottesloe Beach (p106): sit down, grab a snack and take it all in. Kids on body-boards, teens on surfboards, muscle dudes preening, bikini gals parading, dads on stand-up paddleboards, grandads reading the *West Australian*, surf lifesavers surveying the horizon...this is pan-generational people-watching perfection.

❻ Cottesloe Beach Hotel

Follow the sand north a couple of hundred metres to the path leading up to the car park. Cross Marine Pde and veer south to the art-deco **Cottesloe Beach Hotel** (☎08-9383 1000; www.cottesloe-beachhotel.com.au; 104 Marine Pde). There's a good fish restaurant here, but there'll be time for that later: order a drink and head for the fold-back windows, just in time to watch the evening steal the afternoon.

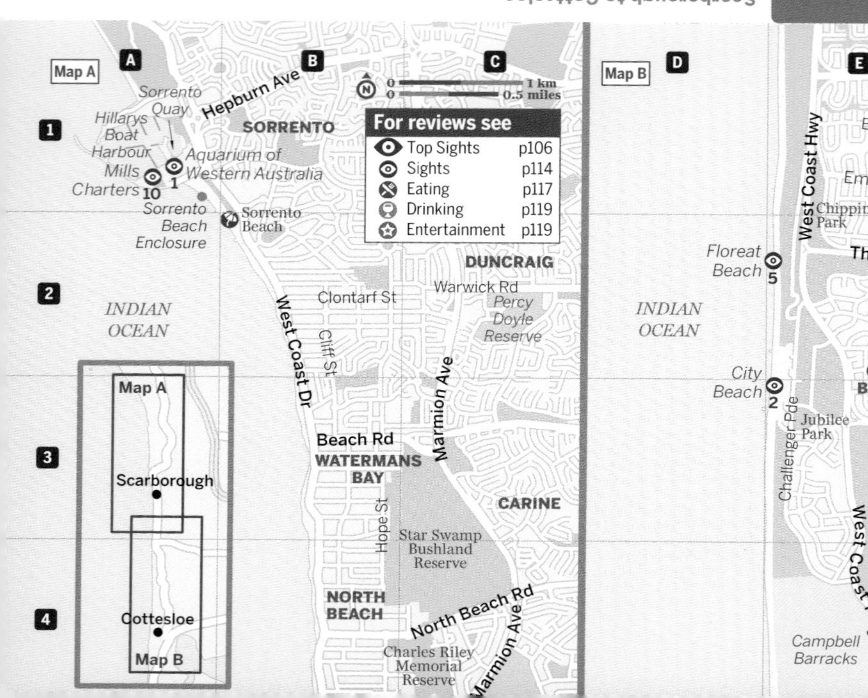

Map A
A
B
C
1 km
0.5 miles
Sorrento Quay
Hepburn Ave
Hillarys Boat Harbour
SORRENTO
Aquarium of Western Australia
Mills Charters 10
1
Sorrento Beach Enclosure
Sorrento Beach
For reviews see
Top Sights p106
Sights p114
Eating p117
Drinking p119
Entertainment p119
DUNCRAIG
Warwick Rd
Clontarf St
Percy Doyle Reserve
INDIAN OCEAN
West Coast Dr
Cliff St
Marmion Ave
Beach Rd
WATERMANS BAY
CARINE
Hope St
Star Swamp Bushland Reserve
NORTH BEACH
North Beach Rd
Charles Riley Memorial Reserve
Map A
Scarborough
Cottesloe
Map B
Map B
D
E
F
Hale Rd
Hale Rd
Weaponess Rd
WEMBLEY DOWNS
Bent St
West Coast Hwy
Empire Ave
Empire Ave
Chipping Park
Durston Rd
Wembley Golf Course
Floreat Beach
5
The Boulevard
INDIAN OCEAN
Kalinda Dr
Bold Park Dr
City Beach
2
CITY BEACH
Oceanic Dr
Challenger Pde
Jubilee Park
Perry Lakes Dr
Bold Park
West Coast Hwy
Stephenson Ave
Rochdale Rd
Campbell Barracks
16
1
2
3
4

A
B
C
D
E
F
5
6
7
8
Mettams Pool
3
West Coast Dr
Trigg Beach
6
TRIGG
West Coast Hwy
Kitchener St
Trigg Bushland Reserve
Hamersley Public Golf Course
St Mary's Anglican Girls' School
Elliott Rd
Coastal Trail
8
Pearl Pde
Scarborough Beach Surf School
Snake Pit
9
Manning St
Scarborough Beach Pool
7
Scarborough Beach Rd
Scarborough Beach
SCARBOROUGH
Brighton Rd
Stanley St
Weaponess Rd
INDIAN OCEAN
Ventnor St
Cobb St
Chipping Park
WEMBLEY DOWNS
Hale Rd
Map continues at top right
Campbell Barracks
West Coast Hwy
Cottesloe Golf Club
Rochdale Rd
MOUNT CLAREMONT
Alfred Rd
Lake Claremont
SWANBOURNE
CLAREMONT
Shenton Rd
Claremont
Swanbourne
Stirling Hwy
12
North St
Allen Park
Swanbourne Beach
4
Grant St
Eric St
COTTESLOE
Broome St
Napier St
McNeil St
Fun's Back Surf
11
John St
Forrest St
Cottesloe Beach
Cottesloe
14
13 PEPPERMINT GROVE
Sea View Golf Course
Curtin Ave
Keane St
Pearse St
Marine Pde
MOSMAN PARK
Mosman Park
Broome St
15
Lochee St

Sights

Aquarium of Western Australia

AQUARIUM

1 MAP P112, A1

Dividing WA's vast coastline into five distinct zones (Far North, Coral Coast, Shipwreck Coast, Perth and Great Southern), AQWA features a 98m underwater tunnel showcasing stingrays, turtles, fish and sharks. (The daring can snorkel or dive with the sharks with the aquarium's in-house divemaster.) By public transport, take the Joondalup train to Warwick Station and then transfer to bus 423. By car, take the Mitchell Fwy north and exit at Hepburn Ave.

Diving and snorkelling with the sharks costs $195. Behind-the-scenes tours ($80 per person) run at 9.45am Friday to Sunday. Bookings are essential. (08-9447 7500; www.aqwa.com.au; Hillarys Boat Harbour, 91 Southside Dr; adult/child $30/18; 10am-5pm)

City Beach

BEACH

2 MAP P112, E3

Offers swimming, surfing, lawn and amenities. Following a significant redevelopment, there are two restaurants (we like Odyssea) and a pizzeria, public change rooms with hot showers and free outdoor seating. On the beach's northern end, old faithful Clancy's pub is another fine option with gorgeous views. Take bus 81 or 82 from Perth Busport. (Challenger Pde)

Surfing at City Beach

Getting into the Waves

If you're feeling at all tentative about swimming in the surf along these ocean beaches (parts of the WA coast do have have a bad rep for shark attacks), detour 9km north of Scarborough to the **Sorrento Beach Enclosure** (Map p112, A1; 08-9400 4000; www.joondalup.wa.gov.au; West Coast Dr; admission free; daylight hours;) – a netted safe-swimming area where you can still feel the waves surge through without the fear of approaching dorsal fins. There's another (more sheltered) safe-swimming area nearby at the **Sorrento Quay Boardwalk** (www.sorrentoquayboardwalk.com.au) – a veritable hive of eating, drinking and shopping activity.

Alternatively, if you're feeling confident (realistically, your chances of becoming something's lunch are utterly minimal – Perth's bus drivers pose more of a threat), sign up for a surf lesson with **Scarborough Beach Surf School** (Map p112, B6; 08-9448 9937; www.surfschool.com; Scarborough Beach; lessons $70; Oct-May). These longer-than-usual lessons (2½ hours) at Scarborough Beach include boards and wetsuits; bookings essential. From June to September the operation moves to Leighton Beach just north of Fremantle.

At Cottesloe, **Fun's Back Surf** (Map p112, D7; 08-9284 7873; 120 Marine Pde; 9am-5pm) hires out stand-up paddleboards ($50 per half-day), surfboards ($25), bodyboards ($20) and snorkelling gear ($20), plus wetsuits ($15) if the brine is a tad brisk.

Mettams Pool

BEACH

3 MAP P112, B5

On calm days, it's like a turquoise paddling pool with some of Perth's best snorkelling – think mottled reef with swaying seaweed and similarly coloured fish. Avoid the water, particularly the outer reef, during rough weather as it has proven dangerous in the past. There's a wheelchair-accessible path leading to a beach shelter and another to the sand. (West Coast Dr;)

Swanbourne Beach

BEACH

4 MAP P112, E6

Safe swimming, and an unofficial nude and gay beach. From Grant St train station it's a 1.5km walk to the beach (2km from Swanbourne Station), or catch bus 102 from Elizabeth Quay Bus Station and get off at Marine Pde. The flashy Shorehouse restaurant has excellent ocean views and a playground out the front. (Marine Pde)

A Tale of Two Cottesloes

Jumping off the train at Cottesloe Station, you'll be forgiven for loudly exclaiming, 'Hey man, where's the beach?' Cottesloe's famous sands are actually 1.5km away to the west: the station sits inland in the suburb's compact commercial zone, which is wedged between the train line and the Stirling Hwy. But before you hightail it to the surf, pause and have a look around. There are some great places to eat and drink here – try Twenty9 (p119) for a coffee and a lovely old pub called the **Albion Hotel** (www.albioncottesloe.com.au), built in 1890, if your thirst extends to something more adventurous. The Boatshed Market (p118) is here too, for picnic supplies. If you don't feel like walking from the station to the beach (or the other way around), Transperth bus 102 connects the two Cottelsoes.

Floreat Beach — BEACH

5 MAP P112, E2

A generally uncrowded beach, but waves can be on the dumpy side. There's decent swimming, surfing, a cafe, playground and a grassy, free BBQ area. Catch bus 81, 82 or 83 from Perth Busport to City Beach and walk north 1km. (West Coast Hwy;)

Trigg Beach — BEACH

6 MAP P112, B6

Good surf, with a hardcore group of locals who come out when the surf's up; it's dangerous when rough and prone to rips – always swim between the flags. Middle Eastern–inspired restaurant Island Market is a fantastic lunch or sunset option, or go more casual at Canteen with poke bowls, next door. (West Coast Hwy)

Scarborough Beach Pool — SWIMMING

7 MAP P112, B7

This superb outdoor, oceanside swimming pool is the place to be when the Fremantle Doctor (p141) blows in and flattens out the Scarborough surf. Bikinis, buff bods, squealing kids and general West Coast ebullience – it's quite a scene. Cafe on-site. (08-9205 7560; www.scarboroughbeachpool.com.au; 171 The Esplanade, Scarborough; swimming adult/child $7/4.30; 5.30am-9pm Mon-Fri, 6.30am-8pm Sat, from 7.30am Sun, reduced hours winter;)

Coastal Trail — CYCLING

8 MAP P112, B6

Feel like a ride? There's a fabulous cycling/walking trail running continuously north from the

Scarborough foreshore, tracing the Indian Ocean clifftops all the way to Hillarys Boat Harbour 10km to the north. The trail extends southwards too, delivering you eventually (with a few detours) to Fremantle, 20km away. (Scarborough Beach Foreshore, Scarborough; admission free)

Snake Pit

SKATING

9 MAP P112, B7

A highlight of the redeveloped Scarborough Beach foreshore is this epic 3.6m-deep concrete skate bowl, named after an open-air rock-and-roll dance joint that stood here in the 1950s. There's also a quarter pipe and stairs, ramps and rails. Do skaters still say 'rad'? (☎08-6557 0700; www.mra.wa.gov.au/see-and-do/scarborough/attractions/snake-pit; The Esplanade, Scarborough; admission free; daylight hours)

Mills Charters

FISHING

10 MAP P112, A1

Epic full-day (or night) fishing trips on the Indian Ocean, chugging out from Hillarys Boat Harbour on Perth's northern shores. (☎08-9246 5334; www.millscharters.com.au; Southside Dr, Hillarys; trips from $199)

Eating

Cott & Co Fish Bar

SEAFOOD $$

11 MAP P112, D7

This sleek seafood restaurant and wine bar is part of the renovated

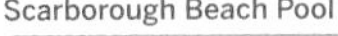

Scarborough Beach Pool

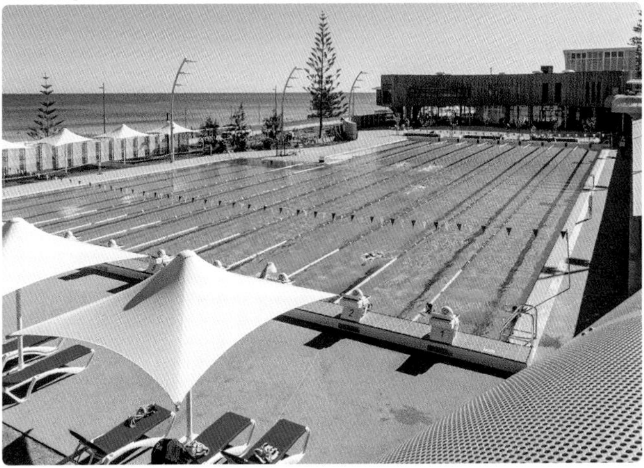

and historic Cottesloe Beach Hotel (p111). Order local oysters and a glass of Margaret River wine, and tumble into a relaxing reverie in front of an Indian Ocean sunset. Out the back, the pub's formerly rowdy garden bar now channels a whitewashed Cape Cod vibe as the Beach Club. (08-9383 1100; www.cottandco.com.au; 104 Marine Pde, Cottesloe; snacks & oysters $3-14, mains $26-41; 5pm-late Wed-Thu, from noon Fri & Sat, to 3pm Sun)

North Street Store BAKERY $

12 MAP P112, E6

If ever you have a hankering for a crispy pork roll or a cinnamon scroll, this is your happy place. Perched on a corner away from the beachfront, this place heaves from early in the morning, not least for its house-baked breads. The coffee is perhaps Cottesloe's best too. (08-9286 2613; www.northstreetstore.com.au; 16 North St, Cottesloe; rolls $10-14; 8am-8pm Mon-Fri, to 3pm Sat & Sun;)

Curtin of Cottesloe

Cottesloe was once home to left-wing Australian prime minister John Curtin, Australia's 14th PM, who held the top job from 1941 until his death in 1945. Before he climbed to the top of the political heap (he's still the only Western Australian to have become PM), Curtin lived at 24 Jarrad St in Cottesloe. The house is now managed by the National Trust; see www.nationaltrust.org.au/initiatives/curtin-family-home-in-safe-hands.

Il Lido ITALIAN $$

Il Lido's al fresco area is popular with Cotteslocals and their dogs, but the sunny interior of this self-styled 'Italian canteen' is arguably even better. It's located close to Cott & Co Fish Bar (see 11 Map p112, D7). Breakfast and coffee attract early-bird swimmers, and throughout the day antipasto plates, house-made pasta and risottos, alongside a thoughtful beer and wine list, continue the culinary buzz. Linger for cocktails and an Indian Ocean sunset. (www.illido.com.au; 88 Marine Pde, Cottesloe; mains $32-42; 7am-late)

Boatshed Market MARKET $$

13 MAP P112, E8

This upmarket, former boatbuilding shed is stacked with fresh produce, aged meat, local fish, deli goods, French pastries and artisanal bread, as well as premade meals including sushi. It's expensive, but the quality is other-level and celebrities such as Elle MacPherson (who runs a business nearby) shop here when they're in town. (08-9284 5176; www.boatshedmarket.com.au; 40 Jarrad St, Cottesloe; 6.30am-8pm)

The Shark Net

For an insight into life along these Perth shores, have a read of Robert Drewe's *The Shark Net* (2000), a haunting recount of adolescence, the beach and disquieting violence. Structured around a macabre series of eight murders that happened here between 1959 and 1963, Drewe's book is as much about Perth society and growing up in these sandy suburbs as it is about Eric Edgar Cooke's rising body count. Cooke was eventually apprehended and became the last person to hang at Fremantle Prison, in 1964. The book also shines a light on the social import of Rottnest Island (p144), a coming-of-age destination for Perth teenagers since well before Drewe first noticed anything particularly interesting about the opposite sex.

Drinking

Twenty9 BAR

14 MAP P112, E7

In the swanky retail street of Cottesloe, away from the chilled-out beach strip, Twenty9 is a casual, family-friendly joint playing Foxtel sport and serving easy-to-please dishes. (08-9284 3482; 29 Napoleon St, Cottesloe; mains $20; 7am-9pm Tue-Wed, to 10pm Thu-Sun)

Entertainment

Camelot Outdoor Cinema CINEMA

15 MAP P112, E8

A seated open-air cinema where you can BYO picnic (no booze). They have free live music ahead of the 8.15pm film screening on Wednesdays, ranging from jazz to folk and blues. (08-9386 3554; http://camelot.lunapalace.com.au; Memorial Hall, 16 Lochee St, Mosman Park; Dec-Easter)

HBF Stadium STADIUM

16 MAP P112, F4

Home to public swimming pools, gym classes and occasional big-ticket music shows. (08-9441 8222; www.hbfstadium.com.au; Stephenson Ave, Mt Claremont)

1897
MUNICIPAL
COUNCIL
FREMANTLE
INFORMATION

Explore Fremantle

Fremantle is a boho harbour town with sea-salty soul to burn – a tight nest of streets with an atmospherically faded cache of Victorian and Edwardian buildings. 'Freo' thrums with live music, craft-beer bars, boutique hotels, left-field bookshops, Indian Ocean seafood shacks, buskers and beaches – it's a fabulous place to spend a few days.

The Short List

- ***Fremantle Prison (p122)*** *Doing time with the ghosts of convicts past in this World Heritage–listed institution.*
- ***WA Shipwrecks Museum (p126)*** *Learning about the 1629 wreck of the* Batavia *and WA's myriad other sea disasters.*
- ***Western Australian Museum – Maritime (p124)*** *Exploring Freo's bonds with the sea.*
- ***Historic Fremantle (p132)*** *Soaking up the faded gold-rush grandeur at the Arts Centre.*
- **Drinking in Fremantle *(p137)*** *Sipping some fine West Australian craft beers.*

Getting There & Away

Fremantle is 30 minutes from Perth Station by train (on the Fremantle line...unsurprisingly).

Bus it from Central Perth: route 103, 107, 111 or 158.

Take a river cruise with Rottnest Express or Captain Cook Cruises.

A cab from Central Perth will cost around $40.

Neighbourhood Map on p130

Fremantle Markets (p132) JASON KNOTT/ALAMY STOCK PHOTO ©

Top Sight

Fremantle Prison

This World Heritage Site is one of Fremantle's most popular places to visit, but don't underestimate how chilling it can be to walk into tiny cells and to see the trapdoors that open up beneath a hanging noose. Going at night further enhances the eerie experience, a very real one for the convicts and prisoners of the day.

MAP P130, D7

www.fremantleprison.com.au

1 The Terrace

day tour adult/child $22/12, combined day tour $32/22, Torchlight Tour $28/18, Tunnels Tour $65/45

9am-5pm

Prison History

With its forbidding 5m-high walls and 6 hectares of bleak yards and imposing buildings, Fremantle's convict-era prison dominates the old town. In the early 1850s, the first convicts here were made to build their own prison, excavating pale limestone blocks from the hill on which it stands. From 1855 to 1991, 350,000 people were incarcerated here, with up to 1200 men and 58 women held at any one time. A staggering 43 men and one woman were executed on-site, the last of which was serial killer Eric Edgar Cooke in 1964 (read about Cooke's despicable exploits in *The Shark Net* (p119), Robert Drewe's excellent 2000 memoir about growing up in Perth in the 1960s).

In 2010 the prison's cultural status was recognised as part of the Australian Convict Sites entry on the Unesco World Heritage list – along with five convict sites in Tasmania, four in New South Wales and one on Norfolk Island.

But it is the prison's location smack-bang in the middle of Freo, and the fact that it remained a fully operational lock-up into the 1990s, that renders it such a potent piece of living history. It's almost impossible to visit Freo without spying the prison walls, and similarly impossible to ignore the fact that thousands of people suffered here: it's no surprise that the prison has a decidedly creepy vibe.

Guided Tours

Various daytime tours explore the jail's maximum-security past, giving insights into criminal minds and allow you into solitary-confinement cells. Book ahead for the Torchlight Tour through the prison, with a few scares and surprises, and the 2½-hour Tunnels Tour (minimum age 12 years), venturing into subterranean tunnels and doing an underground boat ride.

★ Top Tips

- Entry to the gatehouse, including the Prison Gallery, gift shop and Convict Cafe is free.
- If you want to stay the night, book a bed at the excellent **Fremantle Prison YHA Hostel** (☎08-9433 4305; www.yha.com.au; 6a The Terrace; dm $24-29, d & tw from $96, f/cottages from $122/250; 🕑7am-11pm reception; P ❄ 📶 👪) inside the former women's prison and the warden's cottages.

✕ Take a Break

- You could refuel at the **Convict Cafe** (www.fremantleprison.com.au/visit-us/convict-cafe) at a pinch, but its basic menu suggests you might be better off waiting until you return to the Freo cafe strip.

Top Sight

Western Australian Museum – Maritime

This sail-shaped museum is as much about living with the ocean as it is about taming it. Vessels of all descriptions hang from the rafters, from the Australia II *yacht, etched into Australian sporting memory, to old-fangled canoes and pearl-lugging outfits from Broome in WA's north.*

MAP P130, A7

1300 134 081

www.museum.wa.gov.au

Victoria Quay

adult/child museum $15/free, submarine $15/7.50

9.30am-5pm

Galleries & Highlights

The museum has a 11 permanent galleries, focusing on everything from Swan River ferries to fishing, the navy, cargo and the Indian Ocean. But the two undisputed highlights are the famous yacht *Australia II* and the Oberon-class submarine HMAS *Ovens*.

When *Australia II* won the America's Cup yacht race (www.americascup.com) in 1983, Australian Prime Minister Bob Hawke opined, 'Any boss who sacks a worker for not turning up today is a bum'. Indeed, the victory was cause for national celebration, especially in Fremantle, the home of all things maritime in WA. Eyeball the yacht in the 'Tin Canoe to Australia II Gallery', with it's secret weapon – the 'winged keel' – now on not-so-clandestine display (it was hidden behind 'modesty skirts' whenever the boat was out of the water in 1983).

Just as fascinating is the sleek black submarine the HMAS *Ovens*, sitting high and dry on the museum's historic WWII slipway. The *Ovens* was part of the Australian Navy's fleet from 1969 to 1997 – a genuine Cold War relic – and housed 63 submariners in what can generously be described as 'tight' conditions. One-hour tours leave every half-hour from 10am to 3.30pm. Book ahead.

Vintage Van

A classic 1970s Aussie panel van is another crowd-pleaser – because of its status as the surfer's vehicle of choice. The 'pannie' – basically a regular car (a Holden, more often than not) with a roomy cabin on the back – had plenty of space for a surfboard, a guitar, a mattress and a box of beer. High-end interior design often involved fur lining, a disco ball, a fridge unit and a kickin' stereo – everything a young surfer might need for a surfing safari or, after a long day in the waves, the possibility of some horizontal company.

★ Top Tips

- Entry to the WA Maritime Museum is by donation on the second Tuesday of every month.
- Zero in on the *Australia II*, the yacht that won the America's Cup in 1983, ending 132 years of US reign – purportedly the longest winning streak in the history of sport.
- It's well worth taking a guided tour of the Oberon class submarine HMAS *Ovens*.

Take a Break

- The museum has a decent in-house cafe, or it's just a short amble back to central Freo with its myriad eating options. We're big fans of Manuka Woodfire Kitchen (p134) and Ootong & Lincoln (p134).

Top Sight

WA Shipwrecks Museum

Inside an 1852 commissariat store, the WA Shipwrecks Museum is considered the finest display of maritime archaeology in the southern hemisphere. The highlight is the 'Batavia Gallery', featuring a section of the hull of Dutch merchant ship Batavia*, wrecked on the WA coast in 1629. And if you're into maps and how they've changed over time, this is the place for you.*

MAP P130, B7

1300 134 081

www.museum.wa.gov.au

Cliff St

suggested donation $5

9.30am-5pm

Dutch Destinations

Most authorities believe that the first European to spy Aboriginal Australia was Dutchman Willem Janszoon. In 1606 he sailed the *Duyfken* from Batavia (modern Jakarta) to scout for the Dutch East India Company, and found Cape York, which he presumed was part of New Guinea.

Ten years later, another Dutch ship, the *Eendracht,* rode the Atlantic trade winds towards the 'spice islands' (Indonesia). But the captain, Dirk Hartog, misjudged his position and stumbled onto the island (near Gladstone) that now bears his name. Hartog inscribed the details of his visit onto a pewter plate and nailed it to a post. In 1697 the island was visited by a second Dutch explorer, Willem de Vlamingh, who swapped Hartog's plate for one of his own. Both de Vlamingh's battered dish and Hartog's (a replica) are on display at the museum.

The Wreck of the Batavia

Several other Dutch ships came to grief on the uncharted west coast. The most infamous of these was the *Batavia*. After the ship foundered off modern-day Geraldton in 1629, the captain, Francis Pelsaert, sailed a boat back to Batavia for help. In his absence, some crewmen unleashed a nightmare of debauchery, rape and murder on the survivors of the wreck – like something out of *Lord of the Flies*. When Pelsaert returned with a rescue vessel, he executed the murderers, sparing only two youths whom he marooned on the beach of the continent they called 'New Holland'. Some experts believe the legacy of these boys can be found in the sandy hair and Dutch-sounding words of some local Aboriginal people.

Alongside the *Batavia's* waterlogged hull, the museum also displays an ancient stone gate. Salvaged from the wreck, it was intended to be the entrance to Batavia Castle.

★ Top Tips

- Entry is free but a $5 donation is appreciated.
- A Highlights Tour runs daily at 10.30am and 2.30pm and is part of your entry ticket cost.

Take a Break

- There's no on-site cafe at the museum, but the super-popular Little Creatures (p137) craft-beer brewery is just across the road (great pizzas, even better pale ale), as is the hard-to-resist fish and chippery, **Kailis' Fish Market Café** (www.kailis.com/fremantle). Unlike the survivors of the wreck of the *Batavia,* you won't go hungry.

Walking Tour

Fremantle on Foot

Check Fremantle's big-ticket sights off your holiday hit list on this atmospheric amble through the old town. Soak up some nautical vibes en route, plus a few rewarding ales overlooking Fishing Boat Harbour afterwards. As the sun sets over the Indian Ocean, there are few more pleasant places to be.

Walk Facts

Start Monument Hill; Red CAT bus

End Little Creatures; Blue CAT bus

Length 4km; two hours

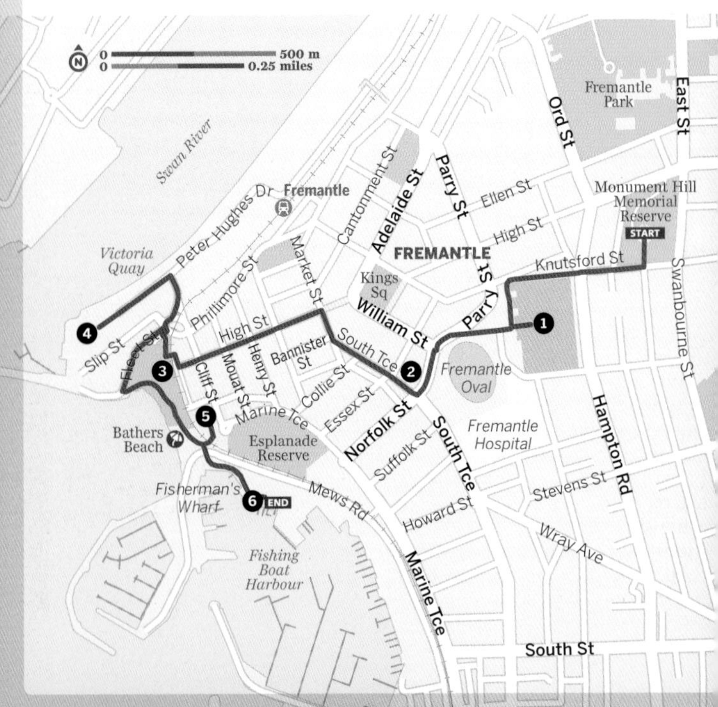

❶ Fremantle Prison

Get the lie of the land (and sea) from atop Monument Hill, a surprisingly steep peak just east of the old town. Take a deep breath of sea air then head downhill to Knutsford St, turn right and cross Hampton Rd. The towering limestone walls of Fremantle Prison (p122) are ahead; slink around the base of the north wall to the entrance on The Terrace. Tours of this astonishing World Heritage–listed jail, fully operational until 1991, are grimly fascinating.

❷ Fremantle Markets

From the front of the prison, take Fairburn St to Parry St past the historic Fremantle Oval (home to the Fremantle Dockers women's team), then turn right onto South Tce, dubbed 'Cappuccino Strip' in less cosmopolitan days (the name has stuck). The historic Fremantle Markets (p132) are on your right: duck inside for a browse, a quick-fire bite and an earful of buskers.

❸ Round House

Continue along South Tce and turn left on High St, the heart of the West End, lined with atmospherically weathered Victorian and Edwardian port buildings. At the end of the street over the rail line is the 1831 Round House (p133), a former prison and WA's oldest building. As per Fremantle Prison, many people endured horrific conditions here; the vibe isn't exactly cheery.

❹ Western Australian Museum – Maritime

Stay west of the rail line, following it around to Peter Hughes Dr and the excellent Western Australian Museum – Maritime (p124) on Victoria Quay. There's an impressive collection of ocean-going craft here, from an Aboriginal canoe to a giant submarine – illuminating Freo's timeless bond with the sea. Don't miss the famous yacht *Australia II*.

❺ WA Shipwrecks Museum

Backtrack to Peter Hughes Dr, veer right onto Fleet St and head down to Bathers Beach – the only beach in WA with an alcohol licence. Abstain for now and follow the foreshore south. Cross the rails again to the excellent WA Shipwrecks Museum (p126), a captivating space in which to wreck a few hours.

❻ Little Creatures

Recross the rail line and follow the waterside boardwalk around Fishing Boat Harbour to Little Creatures (p137), one of Australia's pioneering craft-beer breweries and the perfect spot to end your hike with a pizza and a pale ale. The staff here are achingly hip and as good-looking as the harbour views: do your best not to swoon in admiration.

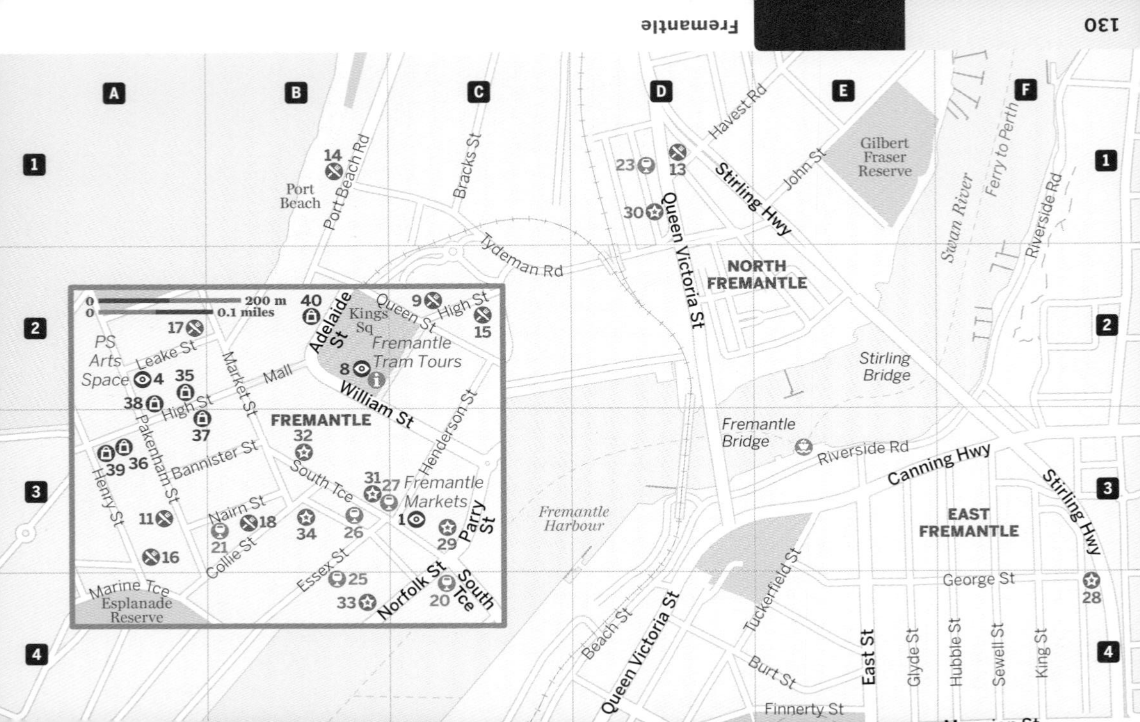

Queen Victoria St
Stirling Hwy
Canning Hwy
NORTH FREMANTLE
EAST FREMANTLE
FREMANTLE
Swan River
Ferry to Perth
Riverside Rd
Gilbert Fraser Reserve
John St
Havest Rd
Stirling Bridge
Fremantle Bridge
Fremantle Harbour
Tuckerfield St
George St
King St
Sewell St
Hubble St
Glyde St
East St
Finnerty St
Burt St
Beach St
Tydeman Rd
Bracks St
Port Beach Rd
Port Beach
Kings Sq
Queen St
High St
Fremantle Tram Tours
Adelaide St
William St
Henderson St
Parry St
Fremantle Markets
South Tce
Norfolk St
Essex St
Collie St
Nairn St
Bannister St
Market St
Mall
Pakenham St
Leake St
Henry St
Marine Tce
Esplanade Reserve
PS Arts Space
200 m
0.1 miles

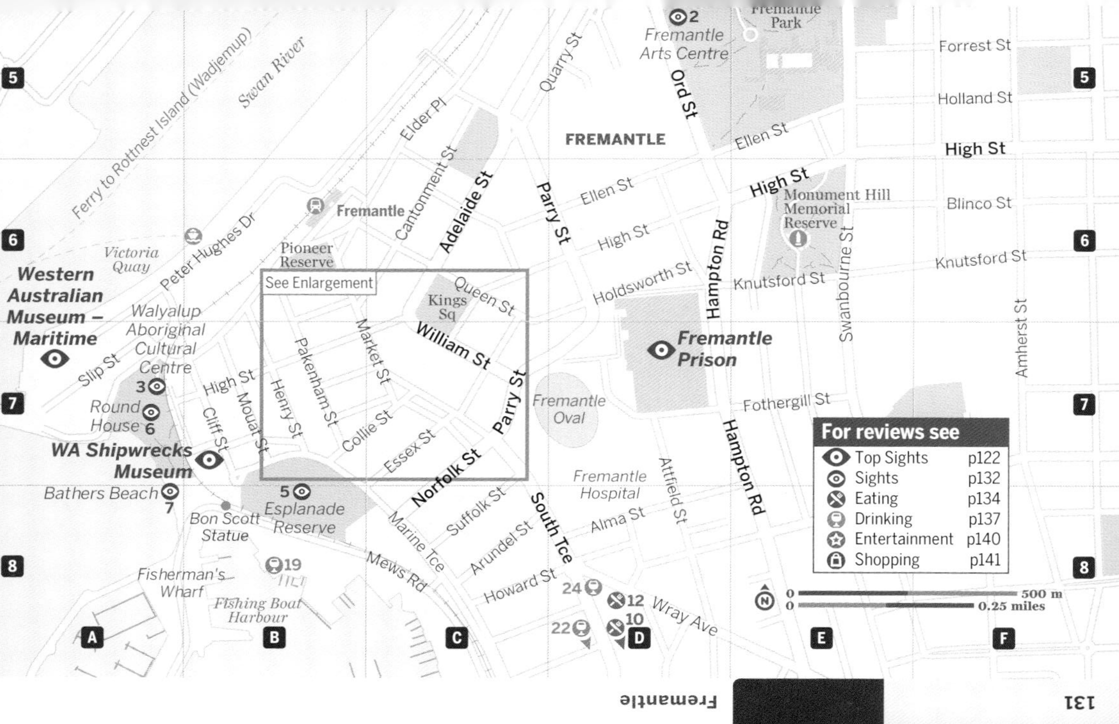

For reviews see
Top Sights p122
Sights p132
Eating p134
Drinking p137
Entertainment p140
Shopping p141
0 500 m
0 0.25 miles
FREMANTLE
Western Australian Museum – Maritime
WA Shipwrecks Museum
Fremantle Prison
Fremantle Arts Centre
Fremantle Park
Monument Hill Memorial Reserve
Walyalup Aboriginal Cultural Centre
Round House
Bathers Beach
Bon Scott Statue
Esplanade Reserve
Fisherman's Wharf
Fishing Boat Harbour
Victoria Quay
Pioneer Reserve
Kings Sq
See Enlargement
Fremantle Oval
Fremantle Hospital
Fremantle
Ferry to Rottnest Island (Wadjemup)
Swan River
Peter Hughes Dr
Slip St
High St
Cliff St
Mouat St
Henry St
Pakenham St
Market St
Collie St
Essex St
Norfolk St
William St
Queen St
Parry St
Adelaide St
Cantonment St
Elder Pl
Quarry St
Ord St
Ellen St
Holdsworth St
Hampton Rd
Knutsford St
Swanbourne St
Fothergill St
Attfield St
Alma St
South Tce
Suffolk St
Arundel St
Howard St
Marine Tce
Mews Rd
Wray Ave
Forrest St
Holland St
Blinco St
Amherst St

Sights

Fremantle Markets

MARKET

1 MAP P130, C3

Originally opened in 1897, these colourful markets were reopened in 1975 and today draw slow-moving crowds combing over souvenirs. A few younger designers and artists have introduced a more vibrant edge. The fresh-produce section is a good place to stock up on supplies and there's an excellent food court featuring lots of global street eats. (www.fremantlemarkets.com.au; cnr South Tce & Henderson St; admission free; 8am-8pm Fri, to 6pm Sat & Sun)

Fremantle Arts Centre

GALLERY

2 MAP P130, D5

An impressive neo-Gothic building surrounded by lovely elm-shaded gardens, the Fremantle Arts Centre was constructed by convict labourers as a lunatic asylum in the 1860s. Saved from demolition in the 1960s, it houses interesting exhibitions and the excellent **Canvas** (08-9335 5685; www.fac.org.au/about/cafe; mains $16-28; 8am-3pm Mon-Fri, to 4pm Sat & Sun;) cafe. During summer there are concerts (free on Sunday afternoons), courses and workshops. (08-9432 9555; www.fac.org.au; 1 Finnerty St; admission free; 10am-5pm)

Ferris wheel, Esplanade Reserve

Walyalup Aboriginal Cultural Centre CULTURAL CENTRE

3 MAP P130, A7

Various classes and workshops, including language, art and crafts, are held at this interesting Aboriginal cultural centre. Booking ahead for most is encouraged, so check the program online. As it's part of the **Bathers Beach Art Precinct** (www.facebook.com/bathersbeach artsprecinct; hours vary) there are also regular Aboriginal art exhibitions, with works available for purchase and proceeds going directly to the artists. (08-9430 7906; www.fremantle.wa.gov.au/wacc; 12 Captains Lane; 10am-3pm Thu-Sat)

PS Arts Space ARTS CENTRE

4 MAP P130, A2

Independent WA artists display often-challenging work in this repurposed heritage warehouse. Occasional events, including pop-up opera, fashion shows and concerts, fill the spacious interior after dark. Drop by or check the Facebook page for what's on. (08-9430 8145; www.facebook.com/pg/pakenhamstreetartspace; 22 Pakenham St; gallery 11am-4pm Tue-Sat)

Esplanade Reserve PARK

5 MAP P130, B8

A large park shaded by Norfolk Island pines between the city and Fishing Boat Harbour. Attractions include a soaring Ferris wheel and a skateboard park. Live-music gigs and festivals are often held here. (Esplanade Park; Marine Tce)

Round House HISTORIC BUILDING

6 MAP P130, A7

Completed in 1831, this 12-sided stone prison is WA's oldest surviving building. It was the site of the colony's first hangings, and was later used for holding Aboriginal people before they were taken to Rottnest Island. At 1pm daily, a time ball and cannon-blasting ceremony just outside re-enacts a historic seamen's alert. Book ahead to fire the cannon.

To the Indigenous Noongar people, this is a sacred site because of the number of Aboriginal people killed while incarcerated here. Freedom fighter Yagan was held here briefly in 1832. Beneath is an impressive 1837 Whalers' Tunnel carved through sandstone and used for accessing Bathers Beach, where whales were landed and processed. (08-9336 6897; www.fremantleroundhouse.com.au; Captains Lane; admission by donation; 10.30am-3.30pm)

Bathers Beach BEACH

7 MAP P130, A8

In late 2016, Bathers became the first beach in WA to be granted an alcohol licence – you can drink cocktails on the sand if you're in a deckchair in front of **Bathers Beach House** (08-9335 2911; www.bathersbeachhouse.com.au; 47 Mews Rd; mains $22-36, grazing boards $49-78; 11am-late;) restaurant.

It's the closest beach to central Fremantle and also has an art trail. You can swim here, but **South Beach** (Ocean Dr) or **Port Beach** (Port Beach Rd) are nicer options.

Fremantle Tram Tours BUS

8 MAP P130, B2

Looking like a heritage tram, this bus departs from the Town Hall on an all-day hop-on, hop-off circuit around the city. The Ghostly Tour, departing 6.45pm and returning 10.30pm Friday, visits the prison (p122), Round House (p133), Fremantle Arts Centre (p132; a former asylum) and the Fremantle Cemetery (p136) – where AC/DC rocker Bon Scott is buried – by torchlight.

Combos include Lunch and Tram (tram plus a lunch cruise on the river; adult/child $92/55), Triple Tour (tram, river cruise and Perth sightseeing bus; $90/26) and Prison Combo (tram plus Fremantle Prison; $45/13). (08-9473 0331; www.fremantletrams.com.au; City Circuit adult/child $27/4, Ghostly Tour $85/65)

Eating

Manuka Woodfire Kitchen BARBECUE, PIZZA $$

9 MAP P130, C2

Relying almost exclusively on a wood-fired oven, the kitchen at Manuka is tiny, but it's still big enough to turn out some of the tastiest food in town. The passionate chef has become an expert at taming the flame; his seasonal menu could include whole roasted fish, coal-grilled eggplant or peppers and basil pesto. The pizzas are also excellent.

A proudly local drinks menu includes Margaret River wine, cocktails using craft gin from Perth and beers from WA's Nail Brewing. The Red Ale is a hoppy marvel. (08-9335 3527; www.manukawoodfire.com.au; 134 High St; shared plates $7-38, pizzas $19-22; 5-9pm Tue-Fri, noon-3pm & 5-9pm Sat & Sun)

Ootong & Lincoln CAFE $$

10 MAP P130, D8

Catch the free CAT bus to South Fremantle for this top breakfast spot. Join the locals grabbing takeaway coffee or beavering away on their laptops, and start the day with macadamia-and-dukkah porridge, or pop in from noon for Mexican corn croquettes. Vintage 1960s furniture and loads of space make it a great place to linger. (08-9335 6109; www.facebook.com/ootongandlincoln; 258 South Tce; mains $12-23; 6am-5pm;)

Bread in Common BISTRO, BAKERY $$

11 MAP P130, A3

Be lured by the comforting aroma of the in-house bakery before staying on for cheese and charcuterie platters, or larger dishes such as lamb ribs, octopus or pork belly. The focus is equally

Fremantle Walking Tours

Operated by a young, energetic crew, **Two Feet & a Heartbeat** (1800 459 388; www.twofeet.com.au; per person $45-99; 10am) focus on Fremantle's often-rambunctious history. The three-hour 'Sailors' Guide to Fremantle' option includes a couple of drink stops, while the 'Convicts and Colonials' tour is an excellent way to get to know the area's key sights. There's also a foodie tour.

Pick up trail cards from the visitor centre (p154) or find them online for 11 self-guided **walking tours** (www.fremantlestory.com.au/explore): there's a street-art trail; one on pubs, past and present; and another covering retro and vintage shops. Local heritage, creativity and Aboriginal history are also covered. Kick off with the discovery trail, covering major tourist attractions. Most walks take less than an hour.

on comfort food and culinary flair, while big shared tables and a chic warehouse ambience encourage conversation over WA wines and Aussie craft beers and ciders. (08-9336 1032; www.breadincommon.com.au; 43 Pakenham St; shared platters $15-19, mains $23-33; 11.30am-10pm Mon-Fri, 8am-late Sat & Sun;)

Little Concept CAFE $

12 MAP P130, D8

Part of the Wray Ave cafe scene, the Little Concept is popular with Freo locals popping in for smoothies, excellent breakfast wraps and stonking slabs of frittata. If you're feeling a tad over coffee, choose from a wide range of flavoured teas, chais and even beetroot latte. Lots of raw and vegan options make this a healthy choice too. (08-6323 1531; www.facebook.com/thelittleconcept; 7 Wray Ave; snacks & mains $10-18; 6.30am-4.30pm Mon-Fri, 7am-4pm Sat, to 3pm Sun;)

Propeller CAFE $$

13 MAP P130, D1

A blue shipping container doubles as a coffee-window and bar inside this sunny cafe-bistro in North Fremantle, enclosed in glass from sometimes icy winds. Middle Eastern flavours inform dishes including Moorish skewers, refreshing salads, and rustic wood-fired *manoushe* (Lebanese flatbreads) spread with lamb, yogurt and pomegranate, or mushroom and blue cheese. The chef's $49 menu is a steal. (08-9335 9366; www.propellernorthfreo.com.au; 222 Queen Victoria St, North Fremantle; shared plates & mains $12-36; 8am-late)

Rockin' Bon Scott

Legendary hell-raiser and front man of Australian hard-rock band AC/DC, Ronald Belford Scott (1946–80), known universally as 'Bon', moved to Fremantle from Scotland with his family in 1956. He spent his teen years strutting around Freo, and the city still adores him.

Down by Fishing Boat Harbour, check out Bon's **statue** (Map p130, B8; Carrington St & Leach Hwy, Palmyra) by local artist Greg James, in classic rock pose (it's a petite rendition – surely not life-size?). Bon's ashes are interred in **Fremantle Cemetery**: enter near the corner of High and Carrington Sts – Bon's plaque is 15m along the path on the left.

Coast

AUSTRALIAN **$$**

14 MAP P130, B1

A breezy laneway fluttering with green fern walls heralds the entry to Coast, a sprawling, multizoned bar-cafe and kiosk that oozes chilled beach vibes with views to match. Perched on Port Beach's fluffy sands, the airy joint's hottest seats are window-facing couches. Best visited for a post-swim lunch or blushing sunset, expect pub-grub, Asian classics and pizza.

What you're wearing might define your visit: Coast's main floor is smart but casual; the elevated cocktail bar is more glamorous, particularly by night. If you're on a budget or simply don't want to rub the sugary sand off your bod, order takeaway fish and chips from the kiosk and join the locals for a beach picnic on the shore. (08-9430 6866; www.coastportbeach.com; 42 Port Beach Rd, North Fremantle; mains $19-32, grazing boards $26-70; 11am-9pm Mon-Wed, to late Thu & Fri, from 9am Sat & Sun)

Raw Kitchen

VEGETARIAN **$$**

15  MAP P130, C2

The beautiful warehouse this vegan, organic and sustainable cafe inhabits is less hippy than you might expect. Boost your energy levels in the concrete, brick and beam surrounds with super-healthy but still tasty food. Plant-based dishes naturally feature raw ingredients – think raw pad thai or poke. Hit the boutique for zero waste and plastic-free finds, including eco cosmetics. (08-9433 4647; www.therawkitchen.com.au; 181a High St; mains $17-25; 11.30am-3.30pm Mon-Thu, to 9pm Fri-Sun;)

Moore & Moore

CAFE **$$**

16  MAP P130, A3

An urban-chic cafe that spills into the adjoining art gallery and overflows into a flagstoned courtyard. With great coffee, farm-direct produce, good cooked breakfasts, pastries, wraps, free wi-fi and eclectic armchairs, it's a great place to linger. Expect the company of a few Freo cool kids and an international crew of students studying at Fremantle's University of Notre Dame. (08-9335 8825; www.mooreandmoorecafe.com; 46 Henry St; mains $12-23; 7am-4pm;)

Leake St Cafe

CAFE $

17 MAP P130, A2

Access this compact courtyard space by walking through the **Kakulas Sister deli** (08-9430 4445; www.kakulassister.net.au; 29-31 Market St; 9am-5.30pm Mon-Fri, to 5pm Sat, from 11.30am Sun;), and find some of Freo's best coffee and an ever-changing menu. Healthy flavours could include a salad of roasted eggplant, chickpeas and toasted almonds, sourdough sandwiches, or good-value brown-rice bowls overflowing with Asian spiced chicken. Don't miss the savoury muffins, especially if figs are in season. (www.facebook.com/pg/leakestcafeteria; Leake St; mains $10-15; 7.30am-3.30pm Mon-Fri)

Duck Duck Bruce

CAFE $$

18 MAP P130, B3

Out of the ordinary breakfast dishes are served in this airy, homey cafe that's flanked with al fresco spaces. Think stewed strawberries and rhubarb over maple granola. Or coconut sambal with eggs and cumin raita. Then there's the vanilla pancake stack with almonds and burnt orange curd. Get there before the 11.30am breakfast cut-off. Dogs are welcome too. (08-6219 5216; www.duckduckbruce.com.au; 8 Collie St; dishes $14-23; 6.30am-3pm Mon-Fri, from 7am Sat & Sun;)

Drinking

Little Creatures

BREWERY

19 MAP P130, B8

Try everything on tap – particularly the Pale Ale and Rogers. The floor's chaotic and fun, and the wood-fired pizzas ($20 to $24) are worth the wait. Shared plates ($8 to $27) include kangaroo with tomato chutney and marinated octopus. There's a sandpit out the back for kids and free bikes for all, plus regular brewery tours ($20). No bookings. (08-6215 1000; www.littlecreatures.com.au; Fishing Boat Harbour, 40 Mews Rd; 10am-late Mon-Fri, from 9am Sat, to 11pm Sun;)

Adventure World

Beer, students and Fremantle: it's all very simpatico. But a night spent mooching between the pubs, breweries and bars here is about more than just drinking beer. The Freo vibe is free-wheeling, breezy and uncomplicated, infused with conversation and live music. Anonymous in the night on this forgotten rim of the planet, if you can't get a little perspective on your life, love and longevity here, there's something amiss!

Norfolk Hotel

PUB

20 MAP P130, C4

Slow down to Freo pace at this 1887 pub. Interesting guest beers wreak havoc for the indecisive drinker, and the food and pizzas are very good. The heritage limestone courtyard is a treat, especially when sunlight dapples through elms and eucalypts. Downstairs, the **Odd Fellow** channels a bohemian small-bar vibe and has live music Wednesday to Saturday from 7pm. (08-9335 5405; www.norfolkhotel.com.au; 47 South Tce; share plates $9-24, mains $19-40; 11am-midnight Mon-Sat, to 10pm Sun)

Strange Company

COCKTAIL BAR

21 MAP P130, B3

Fabulous cocktails – try the spiced daiquiri – WA craft beers and slick, good-value food make Strange Company a sophisticated alternative to the raffish pubs along South Tce. It's still very laid-back, though – this is Freo, after all – and after-work action on the sunny terrace segues into after-dark assignations in Strange Company's cosy wooden interiors. It's worth staying for dinner. (www.strangecompany.com.au; 5 Nairn St; small plates $9-15, mains $14-23; noon-midnight)

Little Creatures (p137)

Percy Flint's Boozery & Eatery

BAR

22 MAP P130, D8

A relaxed neighbourhood watering hole, Percy Flint is very popular with locals. The tap-beer selection is one of Freo's most interesting, with brews from around WA, and shared plates with Mediterranean or Asian flavours are best enjoyed around the big tables in the garden courtyard. (08-9430 8976; www.facebook.com/percyflintsouthfreo; 211 South Tce; 4pm-midnight Tue-Thu, from noon Fri-Sun)

Mrs Browns

BAR

23 MAP P130, D1

Exposed bricks and a copper bar combine with retro and antique furniture to create North Fremantle's most atmospheric drinking den. The music could include all those cult bands you thought were *your* personal secret, and an eclectic menu of beer, wine and tapas targets the more discerning, slightly older bar hound. Ordering burgers from **Flipside** (08-9433 2188; www.flipsideburgers.com.au; 239 Queen Victoria St; burgers $8-16; 11.30am-9pm) next door is encouraged. (08-9336 1887; www.mrsbrownbar.com.au; 241 Queen Victoria St, North Fremantle; 4.30pm-midnight Mon-Thu, from noon Fri & Sat, to 10pm Sun)

Who's Your Mumma

BAR

24 MAP P130, D8

Industrial-chic light bulbs and polished-concrete floors are softened by recycled timber at chilled Who's Your Mumma. An eclectic crew of South Freo locals gathers for excellent cocktails, craft beer and moreish bar snacks, including duck spring rolls and steamed pork buns. (08-9467 8595; www.facebook.com/whosyourmummabar; cnr Wray Ave & South Tce; 4pm-midnight Mon-Thu, from noon Fri & Sat)

Whisper

WINE BAR

25 MAP P130, B4

In a lovely heritage building, this classy French-themed wine bar also does shared plates of charcuterie and cheese. (08-9335 7632; www.whisperwinebar.com.au; 1/15 Essex St; 3pm-late Tue-Thu, from noon Fri-Sun)

Monk

MICROBREWERY

26 MAP P130, B3

Park yourself on the spacious front terrace or in the sturdy interior, partly fashioned from recycled railway sleepers, and enjoy the Monk's own brews (kolsch, mild, wheat, porter, rauch, pale ale). The bar snacks and pizzas are also good, and guest beers and regular seasonal brews always draw a knowledgeable crowd of local craft-beer nerds. (08-9336 7666; www.themonk.com.au; 33 South Tce; 11am-late)

Sail & Anchor
PUB

27 MAP P130, B3

Built in 1854, this historic Fremantle landmark helped start the Australian craft-beer movement a couple of decades ago, but the venerable Sail & Anchor has lost some lustre over recent years. It's still worth checking out to see what's on tap, but there are too many other better pubs in Freo for it to be a must-visit destination. (08-9431 1666; www.sailandanchor.com.au; 64 South Tce; 10am-11pm Mon & Tue, to midnight Wed & Thu, to 1am Fri & Sat, to midnight Sun)

Entertainment

Duke of George
JAZZ

28 MAP P130, F4

Opening in early 2019 in the historic Brush Factory, this is a fun, lively, hugely approachable new jazz bar where dancing between the tables (there's no designated dance floor) is encouraged. Saturday's dinner and show is highly recommended (excellent value too), but you can keep things simple with the à la carte menu of dishes inspired by America's deep south. (08-9319 1618; www.dukeofgeorge.com.au; 135 George St, East Fremantle; plates $18-29; dinner show $35-65 plus gig ticket; 5pm-midnight Thu-Fri, from noon Sat, to 10pm Sun;)

Freo.Social
LIVE MUSIC

29 MAP P130, C3

Part live-music haunt, part micro-brewery, part food-truck and beer-garden hang-out, Freo.Social is difficult to pigeonhole. Opening March 2019, the evolving venue with capacity for 550 people fills a historic space in central Fremantle. It favours big-name local talent, from San Cisco to John Butler and the Waifs, but also leans towards the experimental and has DJ sets. (www.freo.social; Parry St, Fremantle; 11am-midnight Wed-Sun;)

Mojos
LIVE MUSIC

30 MAP P130, D1

Local and national bands (mainly Aussie rock and indie) and DJs play at this small place, and there's a sociable beer garden out the back. First Friday of the month is reggae night, every Monday is open-mic night and local music stars on Tuesdays. It's slightly dingy and dog-eared in that I-want-to-settle-in-all-night kind of way. Locals love it. (08-9430 4010; www.mojosbar.com.au; 237 Queen Victoria St, Fremantle; 5.30pm-midnight Mon-Tue, from 5pm Wed, to 1am Thu-Sat, 4-10pm Sun)

Metropolis Fremantle
LIVE MUSIC

31 MAP P130, B3

Metropolis is a mainstream nightclub on weekends, but roughly twice a month it becomes

The Fremantle Doctor

Huh? Who's a doctor? And why are they the only one in Fremantle? No – this medic is actually Perth's famous summer sea breeze, which cools down the city and provides sweet relief to the gasping, sun-stroked locals. The science is simple: the air over Perth heats up in the sunshine and rises into the sky, sucking in cool air from over the Indian Ocean to fill the void – a classic sea-breeze scenario.

The Doctor peaks between noon and 3pm, reaching wind speeds of up to 20 knots (about 37km/h) and blustering as far inland as York by late afternoon. Local tip: hit the beach in the morning, before the Doctor flattens out the surf and blows sand in your face.

a great space to watch a gig, from punk rock to pop-anthem musos. International and popular Australian bands and DJs perform here. (08-9336 1880; www.metropolisfremantle.com.au; 58 South Tce)

Newport Hotel — LIVE MUSIC

32 MAP P130, B3

Local bands and DJs gig out the back from Friday to Sunday, while there's musical bingo and trivia on quieter nights in this nautically themed pub. The **Tiki Beat Bar** is worth a kitsch cocktail or two. (08-9335 2428; www.thenewport.com; 2 South Tce; noon-10pm Mon-Tue, to midnight Wed-Thu, to 1am Fri & Sat, 11am-10pm Sun)

Luna on SX — CINEMA

33 MAP P130, B4

Art-house cinema between Essex and Norfolk Sts. Cheaper tickets on Wednesday ($12/14 before/after 6pm). (08-9430 5999; www.lunapalace.com.au; Essex St; adult/child $20/14.50;)

Hoyts Millennium — CINEMA

34 MAP P130, B3

Blockbuster heaven with cheaper tickets on Tuesday. (08-9466 4920; www.hoyts.com.au; 29 Collie St;)

Shopping

Common Ground Collective — DESIGN

35 MAP P130, A2

An eclectic showcase of jewellery, apparel and design, much of it limited-edition and mainly from local Fremantle artisans and designers. The coffee at the in-house cafe is pretty damn good too. (0418 158 778; www.facebook.com/cmmngrnd; 82 High St; 10am-5pm Mon-Sat, from 11am Sun)

Found

ARTS & CRAFTS

The Fremantle Arts Centre (see 2 Map p130, D5) shop (p132) stocks an inspiring range of WA art and craft, from textiles and jewellery to prints and woodwork. (08-9432 9569; www.fac.org.au/shop; Fremantle Arts Centre, 1 Finnerty St; 9am-5pm)

Japingka

ART

36 MAP P130, A3

Specialising in ethical Aboriginal fine art from WA and beyond. Purchases come complete with extensive notes about the works and the artists who created them. (08-9335 8265; www.japingka.com.au; 47 High St; 10am-5.30pm Mon-Fri, noon-5pm Sat & Sun)

Record Finder

MUSIC

37 MAP P130, A3

A treasure trove of old vinyl, including niche editions and music styles as well as collectibles. (08-9335 2770; www.truelocal.com.au/business/the-record-finder/fremantle; 87 High St; 10am-5pm)

Bodkin's Bootery

SHOES

38 MAP P130, A2

Handcrafted men's and women's boots and hats. Aussie as. (08-9336 1484; www.bodkinsbootery.com; 72 High St; 9am-5.30pm Mon-Thu, to 6pm Fri, to 6.30pm Sat, noon-6pm Sun)

New Edition

BOOKS

39 MAP P130, A3

Celebrating a sunny corner location for the past 30 years, this bookworm's dream has comfy armchairs for browsing, and a superb collection of Australian fiction and nonfiction tomes for sale. Author events, poetry readings and literary launches are common;

Fremantle Dockers

In 1995 the Fremantle Dockers played their first game in the Australian Football League (AFL; www.afl.com.au). Backed by hordes of rabid, purple-clad fans, the Dockers climbed their way to the semi-finals in 2010 and 2012, before a losing cameo in the 2013 Grand Final broke hearts across the port town. In more recent seasons their performance has been middling at best...and despite having the least-catchy theme song in the league, Freo always looks threatening (particularly when they're playing cross-town rivals the West Coast Eagles).

The club is an integral part of the Fremantle scene: look for everyone wearing purple scarves and guernseys (football shirts) on game days from April to September.

Mojos (p140)

check the website for the shop's latest book reviews. (08-9335 2383; www.newedition.com.au; cnr High & Henry Sts; 9am-9pm)

Mills Records

MUSIC

40 MAP P130, B2

Music, including some rarities (on vinyl and CD), instruments from harmonicas to acoustic guitars, and concert tickets. Check out the 'Local's Board' for recordings by Freo and WA acts. (08-9335 1945; www.mills.com.au; 22 Adelaide St; 9am-5.30pm Mon-Fri, to 5pm Sat, from 11am Sun)

Worth a Trip

Rottnest Island

An intriguing isle, 'Rotto' (or Wadjemup) has long been the go-to destination for Perthites. Cycling, snorkelling, fishing, surfing, diving and wildlife-spotting are excellent; although it's just 19km offshore from Fremantle, it feels a million miles away. But there's a grim history here too: around 3700 Aboriginal prisoners were incarcerated here between 1838 and 1931. Rotto today has a disquieting vibe, even on the sunniest of days.

www.rottnestisland.com

☎ 08-9372 9730

Activities

Rottnest is just big enough to make a day's ride a good workout. The ferry companies all hire out bikes and helmets (around $30/15 per adult/childper day). The visitor centre hires out bikes too.

There are 63 beaches here! Protected by a ring of reefs, **The Basin** (off Kings Way; 24hr;) is the most popular spot for swimming (pictured left). Other good swim spots are **Longreach Bay** and **Geordie Bay**, though there are many smaller secluded beaches around the shoreline, including beautiful **Little Parakeet Bay**. See the online beach guide at www.westernaustralia-travellersguide.com/rottnest-island-beaches.html.

The best surf breaks are at Strickland, Salmon and Stark Bays, towards the western end of the island. Hire bodyboards and wetsuits from **Pedal & Flipper** (08-9292 5105; www.rottnestisland.com/see-and-do; cnr Bedford Way & Welch Rd; bikes per half-/full day from $16/30; 8am-6pm); BYO surfboards.

Rottnest is also a top spot for snorkelling and diving, with excellent visibility, warm waters, reefs and shipwrecks. Contact Pedal & Flipper for gear-hire.

Sights & Guided Tours

Most of Rottnest's historic buildings, built mainly by Aboriginal prisoners, are grouped around Thomson Bay, where the ferries land. The other sights to see here are mostly natural: beaches, bays and viewpoints.

Aside from the many boat, bus and bike island tours available (see www.rottnestisland.com/tours), **Rottnest Voluntary Guides** (08-9372 9757; www.rvga.asn.au; admission free) runs daily guided walking tours around the main settlement and beyond; check the website for times/destinations, or call the visitor centre.

★ Top Tips

- **Rottnest Island Visitor Centre** (08-9372 9730; www.rottnestisland.com; Thomson Bay; 7.30am-6pm Sat-Thu, to 7pm Fri) Accommodation, maps, directions and general advice.
- There are no cars here: plan on doing a lot of walking and cycling.

Take a Break

Grab a pub meal at the excellent waterside **Hotel Rottnest** (08-9292 5011; www.hotelrottnest.com.au; 1 Bedford Ave; mains $21-35; 11am-late).

★ Getting There

Ferry operators include **Rottnest Express** (www.rottnestexpress.com.au) and **Sealink** (www.sealinkrottnest.com.au). Alternatively, contact **Rottnest Air-Taxi** (www.rottnestairtaxi.com.au/joy-flights) or **Rotorvation Helicopters** (www.rotorvation.com.au).

Island History

The island was originally called Wadjemup (place across the water), but Wadjuk oral history recalls that it was joined to the mainland before being cut off by rising waters. Modern scientists date that occurrence to before 6500 years ago, making these memories some of the world's oldest. Archaeological finds suggest that the island was inhabited 30,000 years ago, but not after it was separated from the mainland.

Dutch explorer Willem de Vlamingh claimed discovery of the island in 1696 and named it Rottenest ('rat's nest' in Dutch) because of the king-sized 'rats' (read: quokkas) he saw there.

From 1838 the island was used as a prison for Aboriginal men and boys from all around the state. At least 3670 people were incarcerated here, in harsh conditions, with around 370 dying (at least five were hanged). Although there were no new prisoners after 1903 (by which time holidaymakers from the mainland had already discovered the island), some existing prisoners served their sentences here until 1931. Even before the prison was built, Wadjemup was considered a 'place of the spirits', and it's been rendered even more sacred to Aboriginal people because of the hundreds of their own, including prominent resistance leaders, who died here. Many avoid it to this day.

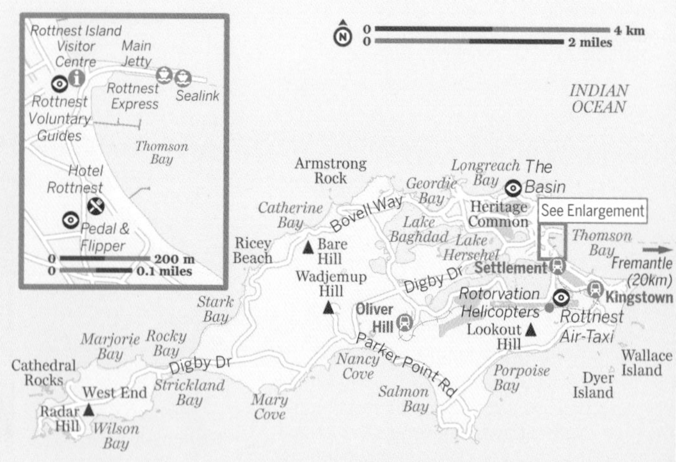

Quokkas

Rottnest's tame little marsupials have suffered over the years. First Willem de Vlamingh's crew mistook them for rats as big as cats. Then the British settlers misheard and mangled their name (the Noongar word was probably *quak-a* or *gwaga*). But, worst of all, a cruel trend of 'quokka soccer' by sadistic louts in the 1990s saw many kicked to death before a $10,000 fine was imposed. On a more positive note, the phenomenon of 'quokka selfies' has illuminated the internet since 2015, and shows no signs of abating (Margot Robbie and Roger Federer in glorious Instagram quokka-company!). Don't be surprised if a quokka approaches looking for a morsel. Politely decline: human food isn't good for them.

During WWI, approximately a thousand men of German and Austrian extraction were incarcerated here, their wives and children left to fend for themselves on the mainland. Ironically, most of the 'Austrians' were actually Croats who objected to Austro-Hungarian rule of their homeland. Internment resumed during WWII, although at that time it was mainly WA's Italian population that was imprisoned.

There's an ongoing push to return the island to its original name. One suggested compromise is to adopt a dual name, Wadjemup/Rottnest.

FRONT
See Cutting Layouts
PATTE
EHOUSE
SALERS
PAPER ONLY

Survival Guide

Street art (p63), Central Perth

CATHERINE SUTHERLAND/LONELY PLANET ©; STREET ART: *LOST GIANT* BY STORMIE MILLS

Before You Go

Book Your Stay

- Perth offers a slew of luxury and designer hotels in Northbridge and the CBD.
- Most of Perth's hostels are in Northbridge.
- Accommodation prices here have fallen of late: Perth is now an affordable place to sleep!

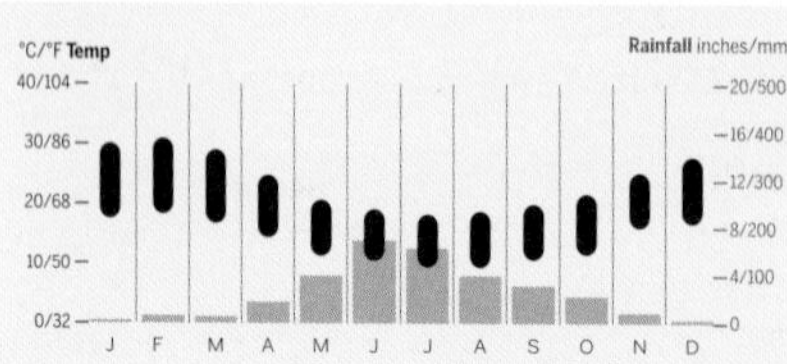

When to Go

- **Feb** The arty Perth Festival is happening and school starts – the beaches begin to empty.
- **Mar** Warm and dry with clear blue skies – perfect beach weather.
- **Sep** Kings Park wildflowers, the Perth Royal Show and the Listen Out festival – what's not to like?

Useful Websites

Lonely Planet (www.lonelyplanet.com/australia/western-australia) Destination information, hotel bookings, traveller forum and more.

Tourism Western Australia (www.westernaustralia.com) Official tourism site; statewide accommodation listings.

Tourism Australia (www.australia.com) Find WA sleeps on the national tourism site.

Best Budget

Hostel G (www.hostel-gperth.com) The newest kid on the Northbridge hostel block is a real game-changer.

Fremantle Hostel (www.fremantlehostel.com.au) Best budget beds down by the harbour in a light-filled former warehouse.

Riverview 42 Mt St Hotel (www.riverviewperth.com.au) Refurbished '60s apartments with retro charm.

Lakeside B&B (www.lakesideperth.com.au) Midrange quality at budget rates in a quiet neighbourhood nook.

Best Midrange

Melbourne Hotel (www.melbournehotel.com.au) The old Melbourne Hotel has been reborn as dynamic boutique winner.

Alex Hotel (www.alexhotel.com.au) The hippest place to stay in Perth, right in the Northbridge action.

Fremantle Apartment (www.thefremantleapartment.com) A NYC-style loft in Freo's heritage precinct.

Cottesloe Beach Hotel (www.cottesloebeachhotel.com.au) Art-deco vibes, sunset beers and maybe a seafood dinner.

Best Top End

Como the Treasury (www.comohotels.com/thetreasury) Simply one of the world's finest hotels.

Westin Perth (www.marriott.com) A slick multinational putting a real local spin on interior design.

QT Perth (www.qthotelsandresorts.com/perth) Stylish, central and unfailingly hip, QT oozes urban cool.

Sebel East Perth (www.thesebel.com/western-australia/the-sebel-east-perth) Away from the city fray, the Sebel is a hushed holiday haven.

Arriving in Perth

Perth Airport

Around 10km east of Perth, **Perth Airport** (www.perthairport.com.au; Airport Dr) is served by numerous airlines.

There are four terminals: T1 and T2 are 15 minutes from T3 and T4. Free transfer buses operates around the clock.

Taxi fares to the city are around $45.

Just Transfers (☎0400 366 893; www.justtransfers.com.au) runs prebooked shuttle-buses between Perth Airport and the city (one way from $25).

Transperth (☎13 62 13; www.transperth.wa.gov.au) bus 40 travels to T3 and T4 and bus 380 runs to T1 and T2, both from Elizabeth Quay Bus Station.

Elizabeth Quay Station

South West Coach Lines (☎08-9753 7700; www.southwestcoachlines.com.au) focuses on the southwestern corner of WA, running services to most towns in the region.

East Perth Station

Transwa (☎13 62 13; www.transwa.wa.gov.au; East Perth Station, West Pde, East Perth; ⏲office 8.30am-5pm Mon-Fri, to 4.30pm Sat, 10am-4pm Sun) operates bus services to/from destinations statewide.

Integrity Coach Lines (Map p36; ☎08-9274 7464; www.integrity-coachlines.com.au; cnr Wellington St & Horseshoe Bridge) runs north–south between Perth and Broome.

Transwa also runs runs train services to/from rural WA:

- *Australind* to Bunbury
- *MerredinLink* to Merredin
- *Prospector* to Kalgoorlie–Boulder

Great Southern Rail (☎1800 703 357; www.greatsouthernrail.com.au) runs the *Indian Pacific* train between Perth and Sydney – a four-day, three-night, 4352km cross-continental epic.

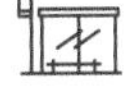

Getting Around

Car & Motorcycle

Some Central Perth streets are one way; many aren't sign-posted. Car rental companies proliferate. There are plenty of car-parking buildings in the central city.

Scootamoré (☎08-9380 6580; www.scootamore.com.au; 356a Rokeby Rd, Subiaco; hire 1/3/7 days $60/150/300; ⏲8.30am-5.30pm Mon-Fri, 9am-1pm Sat) hires out 50cc scooters.

Train

Transperth (13 62 13; www.transperth.wa.gov.au) operates five train lines from around 5.20am to midnight weekdays and to about 2am Saturday and Sunday: Armadale Thornlie, Fremantle, Joondalup, Mandurah and Midland.

Perth Station (13 62 13; www.transperth.wa.gov.au; Wellington St) is the main hub.

Elizabeth Quay Station (13 62 13; www.transperth.wa.gov.au; off William St, Elizabeth Quay) is serviced by the Joondalup and Mandurah lines.

Bus

The Perth metropolitan area and central **Free Transit Zone** (FTZ) are served by regular Transperth buses and four free **Central Area Transit** (CAT) services. Fremantle aslo has two free CATs.

Buses run every five to 15 minutes, and more frequently on weekdays. Digital displays at the stops detail arrivals.

Taxi

Perth has a decent system of metered taxis. Uber also operates throughout Perth.

Swan Taxis (13 13 30; www.swantaxis.com.au)

Black & White Cabs (08-9230 0440; www.blackandwhitecabs.com.au)

Ferry

A Transperth ferry runs every 20 to 30 minutes between **Elizabeth Quay Jetty** (Map p36; 13 62 13; www.transperth.wa.gov.au; off William St, Elizabeth Quay) and South Perth (for Perth Zoo).

Little Ferry Co (Map p36; 0488 777 088; www.littleferryco.com.au; Elizabeth Quay; 1/2/3 stops adult $12/18/22, child $10/16/20, day pass adult/child $32/28; 10am-5.30pm) runs scheduled services linking Elizabeth Quay and Claisebrook Cove, plus Perth Stadium on big-game days.

Rottnest Express (1300 467 688; www.rottnestexpress.com.au) runs ferries to Rottnest Island from both Elizabeth Quay and Fremantle.

Bicycle

Perth has some great bike tracks around the river, Kings Park and coastline: see www.transport.wa.gov.au/cycling.

Spinway WA (0413 343 305; www.spinwaywa.bike; per 1/4/24hr from $11/22/33) has 14 self-serve bicycle-hire kiosks around the city. Bikes cost $11/22/33 per one/four/24 hours. Swipe your credit card and follow the prompts. Helmets and locks included.

Bike rentals:

Cycle Centre (08-9325 1176; www.cyclecentre.com.au; 326 Hay St; bike hire per day/week from $25/65; 9am-5.30pm Mon-Fri, to 4pm Sat, from 1pm Sun)

About Bike Hire (08-9221 2665; www.aboutbikehire.com.au; 305 Riverside Dr, East Perth; per hour/day/week from $10/24/64; 8am-6pm Nov-Mar, reduced hours Apr, May & Oct)

Free Wheeling Fremantle (08-9431 7878; www.fremantle.wa.gov.au/visit/getting-around/cycling; Fremantle Visitor Centre, Kings Sq; 9am-5pm Wed-Sun)

Essential Information

Accessible Travel

- Most theatres, cinemas, cafes and restaurants cater for people with disabilities; finding accessible accommodation is less straightforward.
- See www.transperth.wa.gov.au/about/accessibility for info on accessible public transport.
- Spinal Cord Injuries Australia has accessible accommodation info: http://scia.intersearch.com.au/kohamapdistance.php.

Business Hours

Most Perth attractions close on Christmas Day; many also close on New Year's Day and Good Friday.

Banks 9.30am–4pm Monday to Friday

Cafes 7am–4pm

Pubs and Bars pubs 11am–midnight (food typically noon–2pm and 6pm–8pm), bars 4pm–late

Restaurants lunch noon–2pm, dinner 6pm–9pm (often later)

Shops 9am–5pm Monday to Saturday (to 9pm Friday), 11am–5pm Sunday

Supermarkets 7am or 8am–8pm, some open 24 hours

Electricity

Type I
230V/50Hz

Emergencies

Emergency (police, fire, ambulance)	000
Directory assistance	1223

Perth Police Station

(emergency 000, non-emergency 08-9422 7111; www.police.wa.gov.au; 2 Fitzgerald St; 24hr)

LGBTIQ+ Travellers

- Perth is largely a welcoming and safe destination.
- Pick up the free monthly newspaper *Out in Perth* (www.outinperth.com).

Money

ATMs are plentiful, and there are currency-exchange facilities at the airport and major banks in the CBD.

Credit & Debit Cards

- Visa and MasterCard are widely accepted; Diners Club and Amex not so much.
- Debit cards connected to the international banking network (Cirrus, Maestro, Plus and Eurocard) will work.

Public Holidays

New Year's Day 1 January

Australia Day 26 January

Labour Day First Monday in March

Easter (Good Friday and Easter Monday) March/April

Anzac Day 25 April

Money-saving Tips

If you're in Perth for a while, consider buying a Transperth SmartRider card (www.transperth.wa.gov.au/smartrider), covering bus, train and ferry public transport. It's $10 to purchase, then you add value to your card. Tap in, tap out... It works out 10% to 20% cheaper than buying single tickets.

Western Australia Day First Monday in June

Queen's Birthday Last Monday in September

Christmas Day 25 December

Boxing Day 26 December

Safe Travel

- Perth is generally a safe city, but keep your wits about you in pubs (especially around Northbridge) and on the streets after dark.

Telephone Services

- Australia's two main telecommunications companies are Telstra (www.telstra.com.au) and Optus (www.optus.com.au).
- Mobile (cell) services are provided by Telstra, Optus, Vodafone (www.vodafone.com.au) and Virgin (www.virginmobile.com.au).
- Australia's mobile network is compatible with most European phones, but generally not with the US or Japanese systems.
- The main service providers offer prepaid SIMs.

Tourist Information

Perth City Visitor Kiosk (Map p36; www.visitperth.com.au; Forrest Pl, Murray St Mall; 9.30am-4.30pm Mon-Thu & Sat, to 8pm Fri, 11am-3.30pm Sun) Volunteers here answer questions and run walking tours.

WA Visitor Centre (Map p36; 08-9483 1111; www.wavisitorcentre.com.au; 55 William St; 9am-5pm Mon-Fri, 9.30am-4pm Sat & Sun) Excellent resource for information across WA.

Fremantle Visitor Centre (Map p130; 08-9431 7878; www.visitfremantle.com.au; Town Hall, Kings Sq; 9am-5pm Mon-Fri, to 4pm Sat, from 10am Sun) Accommodation and tour bookings; bike rental.

Visas

All visitors to Australia need a visa – only New Zealand nationals are exempt. Apply via www.homeaffairs.gov.au.

eVisitor (651)

- Many European passport-holders are eligible for a free eVisitor visa, allowing visits to Australia for up to three months at a time within a 12-month period.
- Apply at least 14 days prior to the proposed date of travel to Australia.

Electronic Travel Authority (601)

- Passport-holders from many of the European countries eligible for eVisitor visas, plus passport-holders from Brunei, Canada, Hong Kong, Japan, Malaysia, Singapore, South Korea and the USA, can apply for either a visitor or business ETA.
- ETAs are valid for 12 months, with multiple stays of up to three months permitted.

Behind the Scenes

Send Us Your Feedback

We love to hear from travellers – your comments help make our books better. We read every word, and we guarantee that your feedback goes straight to the authors. Visit **lonelyplanet.com/contact** to submit your updates and suggestions.

Note: We may edit, reproduce and incorporate your comments in Lonely Planet products such as guidebooks, websites and digital products, so let us know if you don't want your comments reproduced or your name acknowledged. For a copy of our privacy policy visit lonelyplanet.com/privacy.

Charles Rawlings-Way

Big thanks to Tasmin for the gig, to Fleur for the inside info on Perth culture, and to all the helpful souls I met on the road in South Australia and in/around Perth who flew through my questions with the greatest of ease. Biggest thanks of all to Meg, who made sure that Ione, Remy, Liv and Reuben were looked after.

Fleur Bainger

Thrilled and grateful to be on board. Thanks to Tasmin and Charles for their endless patience with helping me learn the guidebook writing ropes. Western Australia's epic scenery, passionate characters and inspiring produce also deserve gratitude; they constantly inspire me.

Acknowledgements

Cover photograph: Cottesloe Beach, Hans Peter Huber/4Corners Images ©

Photographs pp26–7 (clockwise from top left): Eden Nguyen/Shutterstock ©, (*Spanda* by Christian de Vietri) bmphotographer/Shutterstock ©, Jason Knott/Alamy Stock Photo ©

This Book

This 1st edition of Lonely Planet's *Pocket Perth & Fremantle* guidebook was researched and written by Charles Rawlings-Way and Fleur Bainger. This guidebook was produced by the following:

Destination Editor Tasmin Waby

Senior Product Editors Kate Chapman, Anne Mason

Regional Senior Cartographer Julie Sheridan

Product Editor Rachel Rawling

Book Designer Meri Blazevski

Assisting Editors Sarah Bailey, Peter Cruttenden, Carly Hall, Victoria Harrison, Kellie Langdon

Cover Researcher Naomi Parker

Thanks to Carolyn Boicos, Paul Harding, Vicky Smith

Index

See also separate subindexes for:
- Eating p158
- Drinking p159
- Entertainment p159
- Shopping p159

Sights 000
Map Pages **000**

Eating

Drinking

Entertainment

Shopping

Our Writers

Charles Rawlings-Way

Charles is a veteran travel, food and music writer who has penned 40-something titles for Lonely Planet plus too many articles to recall. After dabbling in the dark arts of architecture, cartography, project management and busking for some years, Charles hit the road for Lonely Planet in 2005 and hasn't stopped travelling since. He's also the author of a best-selling rock biography on Glasgow band Del Amitri, *These are Such Perfect Days*. Follow Charles on the socials @crawlingsway and www.facebook.com/chasrwmusic.

Fleur Bainger

Having worn her first backpack to Europe when she was just 10 years old, Perth-based journalist Fleur gets a heck of a buzz from being a freelance travel and food writer. As Western Australia's weekly food reviewer for the *Sunday Times Magazine*, she's constantly on the hunt for Perth's best new eateries, while her weekly 'what's on' slot on 6PR talkback radio means she's always got the lowdown on events and openings around town. She's a Lonely Planet Local, a destination expert for the *Telegraph* (UK) and regular contributor to *Australian Traveller, Escape,* ABC radio and more.

Published by Lonely Planet Global Limited
CRN 554153
1st edition – Nov 2019
ISBN 978 1 78868 270 1

10 9 8 7 6 5 4 3 2 1
Printed in Malaysia